JUNE 2022

D0998580

It Takes
Guts

It Takes Guts

HOW YOUR BODY TURNS FOOD INTO FUEL

(AND POOP)

Dr. Jennifer Gardy

ILLUSTRATIONS BY
Belle Wuthrich

GREYSTONE KIDS

GREYSTONE BOOKS • VANCOUVER/BERKELEY

Greystone Kids / Greystone Books Ltd.
greystonebooks.com

Cataloguing data available from Library and Archives Canada
ISBN 978-1-77164-501-0 (cloth)
ISBN 978-1-77164-502-7 (epub)

Editing and indexing by Catherine Marjoribanks
Copy editing by Dawn Loewen
Proofreading by Alison Strobel
Jacket and interior design by Belle Wuthrich
The illustrations in this book were rendered in Adobe Illustrator

Printed and bound in Singapore on ancient-forest-friendly paper
by COS Printers Pte Ltd.

Greystone Books gratefully acknowledges the Musqueam, Squamish,
and Tsleil-Waututh peoples on whose land our office is located.

Greystone Books thanks the Canada Council for the Arts,
the British Columbia Arts Council, the Province of British Columbia
through the Book Publishing Tax Credit, and the Government of Canada
for supporting our publishing activities.

Canadä

Contents

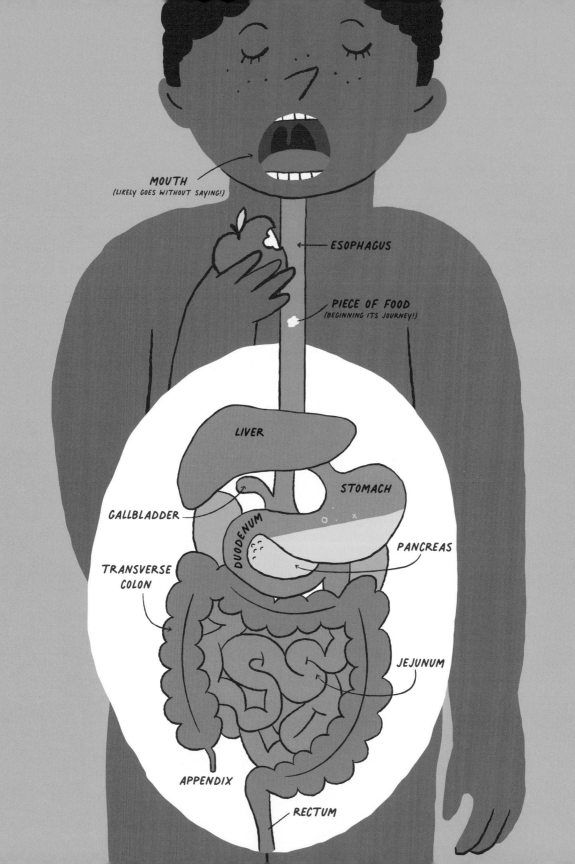

INTRODUCTION

THE —— WONDERFUL —— WORLD OF GUTS

EVERYBODY EATS AND EVERYBODY poops. It might seem ordinary, but what happens between your mouth and your butt is almost magical, and you owe it all to one of the most remarkable parts of your body—your gut. Every day, you turn food into fuel and neatly dispose of the leftovers. Did you know that you produce over a pound (half a kilogram) of poop every day?

This sophisticated system is one of the very first things that developed when you were in the womb. When the embryo that became you was just 16 days old, a simple tube formed from a single layer of cells. As the embryo grew, the tube became more complex. By eight weeks, you had miniature copies of all the organs that make up your gut, or digestive tract. By the time you were born, those organs had almost completely developed—and you'd even formed your very first poop!

As you grow, your gut grows along with you. Eventually it'll measure around 23 feet (7 meters) long—over half as long as a school bus! Every moment of every day of your life, your gut deals with everything you eat and drink: foods and liquids go in one end, the many organs that make up your digestive system take all the healthy nutrients and other useful components out for your body to use, and the rest comes out at the other end as poop. But scientists are learning new things every day about how the gut does so much more for us! It's practically a part of our brain, able to send signals that tell us when we're hungry or full. And it can even influence our mood—imagine being able to change how you feel by eating a different diet.

Our gut is part of our **immune system** too, defending our bodies against dangerous germs. And it's also home to trillions of tiny **bacteria** that live with us in (usually) perfect harmony. They help us with some of the more difficult jobs of digestion, but they also shape how healthy we are. The bacteria present in our first few poops as babies can tell doctors whether or not we might grow up to develop allergies or asthma!

As a scientist who's always wondered exactly what's happening inside me, I've done some wacky things to

understand how my digestive system works—from swallowing a tiny camera to explore my stomach and intestines from the inside, to looking at my own poop under a microscope to see the millions of bacteria living inside me. I've tested my DNA to see why my body reacts to some foods differently than other people's bodies do, and I've changed my diet to see how what I eat affects everything from my mood to how my poop smells! I've learned a lot on the way, but there's still so much more to discover.

So join me as we take an up-close-and-personal look at the secret, scientific, and strange world of our guts.

1.

WHERE IT ALL BEGINS

—— THE MOUTH ——

STAND IN FRONT OF A MIRROR and open wide. What do you see? Lips? The inside of your cheeks? A tongue? Some teeth? They all have an important role to play in getting food into your mouth and into your gut. But there's a lot more going on here than meets the eye. Some of the almost invisible stuff in your mouth actually has a pretty big job to do.

Saliva: A Lovely, Lively Liquid

TAKE SPIT, FOR INSTANCE—OR, to use its scientific name, **saliva**. You make as much as 6 cups (up to 1.5 liters) of saliva every day! What is it? Well, it's 99.5 percent water, but saliva also contains all this stuff:

- Hydrogen peroxide. Commonly used in first aid to disinfect cuts, it works to kill bad bacteria.

- Tiny molecules called *growth factors*. These help microscopic wounds in your mouth to heal.

- Pain-killing molecules six times stronger than a doctor might prescribe. Scientists think these molecules may have helped our early ancestors—who definitely didn't have drugstores—deal with pain.

- A bit of (you're not going to like this) urea, the main ingredient in pee. Urea keeps your mouth from getting too acidic, which can be bad for your teeth.

- **Enzymes**—the most important part of saliva. These molecules start the job of breaking food down into smaller parts for digestion.

THE SURPRISING SOURCE OF SALIVA

Anybody who's ever seen something delicious and started to salivate knows that our bodies can summon saliva at a moment's notice, but do you know where it comes from? It actually has a surprising source... your blood! Saliva is produced by the hundreds of salivary glands in your mouth. Each of these tiny factories is fed by a blood vessel. When blood, which is mostly water, reaches the salivary glands, a special set of cells acts as a sort of filter, straining out all the things, like red blood cells, that are too big to pass through the filter. The water and the small molecules that make it through carry on their journey through the salivary gland and into your mouth, in the form of freshly made saliva.

Most of the enzymes that help you digest your food are found farther down your digestive tract, but the very first steps of digestion actually take place in your mouth. Saliva contains many different enzymes, each of which speeds up a different chemical reaction. So if, for example, you eat food containing fats—like dairy, nuts, or eggs—an enzyme called *lipase* gets to work to break the fats down into smaller molecules that your gut can absorb. If you've

eaten starchy foods, like bread or fries, enzymes called *amylases* step up to the plate.

You'll meet more marvelous enzymes later, but for now, let's look at something else in your mouth. You can't see them, but you can't live without them—millions and millions of microscopic bacteria.

Bacterial Buddies

YOUR MOUTH IS FULL OF BACTERIA, around 300 different types. While some of them are troublemakers, causing bad breath and contributing to cavities and gum disease, most of them are very helpful.

WHAT THE HALITOSIS?

Bad breath, or **halitosis**, is very common. In fact, most of us wake up every morning with a bit of a funky mouth, and we have bacteria to blame. While some bad breath is due to food odor—garlic breath, anyone?—most of it is caused by bacteria that feed on decomposing food. Scientists can use complex machines to identify these bad odors, or they can rely on a simpler—and pretty unusual—solution: people whose job it is to sniff out bad breath! These people have supersensitive noses, which they put to work by recognizing and rating bad breath smells. For example, companies making mouthwash use these so-called odor judges to see how well their product is working.

Scientists knew that our mouths contained bacteria before they even knew what bacteria were! In the 17th century, Antonie van Leeuwenhoek built powerful microscopes by hand, crafting lenses that could magnify things hundreds of times. When he examined plaque scraped from his own teeth, he observed hundreds of tiny cells moving about. He called these *animalcules*, from the Latin word for "little animal," but we know them today as bacteria.

What Do Bacteria Do?

Most of the good bacteria in your mouth have a simple job—to keep bad bacteria out. But your microscopic friends also assist with digestion. Just as we humans produce enzymes that break down our food, so too do bacteria. In fact, because they make enzymes that we don't, some bacteria can break down starches that we couldn't digest on our own. And scientists have discovered that the bacteria in our mouths even work to increase our levels of nitric oxide, a molecule that helps keep our blood flowing effectively.

Chew on This

CAN YOU GUESS WHICH of your muscles is the strongest? Maybe your biceps, which let you lift heavy objects? Or is it your heart, pumping blood throughout your body more than 100,000 times a day? Or maybe your glutes—your butt muscles that power up when you sit and stand and walk? Nope, guess again!

The strongest muscle in your body connects your lower jaw to your cheekbone. It's called the **masseter**, and it's a master of its trade. Place your hands on your cheeks, close your mouth, and clench and unclench your teeth—that muscle you feel moving is your masseter, and it's capable of producing around 200 pounds (90 kilograms) of pressure between your teeth. But chewing isn't just about strength; it involves finesse as well! The moment your teeth make contact with your food and crush it into the right texture, your masseter needs to throw on the brakes—otherwise, you'd smash your teeth together. Few muscles in the human body can stop as quickly and precisely as the jaw muscles!

The nerves that power these mouth muscles also play an important role. They help you detect where in your mouth a piece of food is located, and they are so sensitive that they can pinpoint the location of a particle even smaller than a grain of sand. These nerves also help you determine how much chewing force you need to apply to break your food apart, whether it's a soft marshmallow or a tough nut that you're munching on.

Tooth Talk

Your teeth are pretty impressive too. Tooth enamel is the hardest substance in the human body, harder than bone, and it helps your teeth to withstand the enormous pressure of chewing. Four types of teeth work together to rip apart food, no matter how tough it might be. The incisors, at the front of your mouth, cut food into smaller bites, while your canine teeth—named because they resemble the pointy fangs of a dog—grab and tear your food. Your premolars and molars, the flat teeth toward the back of your mouth, crush and grind your food.

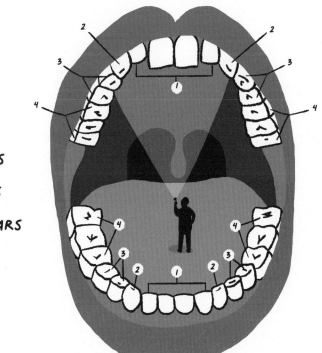

1. INCISORS

2. CANINES

3. PREMOLARS

4. MOLARS

Tongue Twister

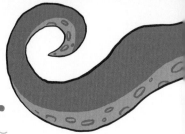

SO FAR, YOU'VE LEARNED that your mouth is home to the strongest muscle in your body and the hardest substance in your body. But wait! There's more! It's also the site of the most flexible muscle in your body—the tongue. The tongue is actually made up of eight different muscles, and it behaves a lot like an octopus's tentacle or an elephant's trunk. That's why your tongue can bend, twist, lengthen, and shorten any which way, helping not only to position food in the mouth, but also to produce the many sounds that make up human speech.

The surface of your tongue is covered with thousands of tiny bumps, and those bumps are covered with thousands of even tinier bumps, invisible to the naked eye. These are your **taste buds**, and each one contains specialized taste receptor cells. As the enzymes in your saliva begin to break down your food, the different types of taste receptors begin to detect different chemicals, giving rise to taste sensations like sweet, salty, or bitter. These sensations combine with the smell of your food, and other things like texture, temperature, and spiciness, which are detected through special nerves that connect your mouth to your brain, creating the complete sensation of eating.

ARE YOU A SUPERTASTER?

The way people taste food is highly individual. Differences in our genetics mean that you and I might experience food very differently. Some people are even **supertasters**, thanks to having more taste buds than usual. Are you a supertaster? With a magnifying glass, a friend, and a bit of blue food coloring, you can find out!

Place a drop of blue food coloring on your tongue and use a mouthful of water to swirl the dye around your mouth. Your tongue should now be mostly blue, except for light blue or pink bumps. These are called *papillae*, and each one is covered in taste buds.

Now use a hole punch to cut a hole in a piece of paper, and place the cutout over your tongue. Have a friend use a magnifying glass to count the papillae visible through the hole. Do this in a few different areas of your tongue, and record your observations. Average tasters will have about 15 to 30 papillae visible through the cutout. More than 30 suggests you might be a supertaster!

It's Not Hard to Swallow

YOU DON'T HAVE TO think about it—somehow your brain just knows when the food in your mouth is small enough that you can stop chewing and start swallowing. Exactly how this happens isn't well understood, but it's thought that the human brain integrates many sensations—muscle movements, the size and texture of the food, how dry it is—to determine when food is safe to swallow. It's a process that people learn by trial and error as very young children, and we practice it a lot—the average person swallows over 2,000 times every day!

When your brain sends the "Swallow now!" signal to your mouth, you press your tongue toward the roof of your mouth. This helps direct the food toward the back of your mouth, but it also serves another important purpose. Ever sneezed a noodle out of your nose? This happens because the nasal passages and the mouth both lead to the same place—the throat, or **pharynx**. Normally, a small piece of tissue—called the **soft palate**, which is located right behind the hard roof of your mouth—acts as a sort of traffic cop. When you're about to swallow, the soft palate closes, blocking the entrance to your nose. That's why you can breathe and swallow, but not at the same time. Sometimes, though, things don't work the way they're supposed to, and a bit of stealthy spaghetti can sneak past the soft palate, only to be violently ejected through your nose when you sneeze.

Just past the soft palate, the throat goes from being one big tube to two separate tubes: one to carry air to your lungs, called the **trachea**, and another to carry food to your stomach—more on that in a moment! Just like a switch that directs a train onto a different track, your **epiglottis**— a small flap of tissue—directs your food toward the proper passage. By covering the entrance to the trachea, the epiglottis sends whatever you've swallowed to your digestive system. But it won't be free-falling toward your stomach. Instead it's about to enter a perfectly practical passage—the food tube, or the **esophagus**.

The Wrong Tube

It's happened to all of us: food or drink going down the wrong tube. (It's usually drink—liquids are messy and move quickly, so it's easy for them to go astray.) Maybe you got distracted for a second, or something startled you at the exact moment you were swallowing. This is called *aspiration*, and it is no fun.

Most of the time, the problem will sort itself out. The presence of an intruder in your airway triggers a cough reflex that usually dislodges the food and sets it back on its proper course. This is why you don't often cough out what you've aspirated: instead of coming back to your mouth, it just makes a U-turn and heads down the esophagus like it was supposed to.

Not being able to clear the culprit can cause trouble, though. If the chunk is large enough, it may block the airway and lead to choking. Food can also enter your lungs and attract bacteria, leading to a lung infection called *pneumonia* that must be treated by a doctor.

Another Nervous System

Next time you swallow a bite of food, take a moment to notice something unusual. When you're swallowing, nothing else is happening. You're not chewing, you can't cough or sneeze, you're not even breathing!

Swallowing is a complex process that requires a lot of coordination—there can't be any distractions. So why don't you normally have to focus all your attention on swallowing? That's thanks to the fact that your digestive system has its very own nervous system, called the **enteric nervous system**. It's so sophisticated that some scientists have taken to calling it the "second brain." Unlike the rest of your body, which requires signals from the brain or spinal cord to function, your gut can operate using the signals it receives from the enteric nervous system alone— no brain required!

BRAIN FREEZE

It's a hot day, and you've just dug into a bowl of delicious ice cream. That first bite hits your palate, but instead of the sheer pleasure of a cold creamy treat on a sweltering summer's day... INSTANT HEADACHE! It feels like a band is being tightened around your skull, and there's nothing you can do but writhe and moan and wait a few seconds for the terrible sensation to pass. What the heck was that?!

Brain freeze, or *sphenopalatine ganglioneuralgia* (don't worry, it's not going to be on the spelling test!), happens when something very cold, like ice cream, comes in contact with the roof of your mouth or the back of your throat. These are typically very warm places, and the dramatic temperature change sounds an alarm—"Something's not right here!"—in your trigeminal nerve, the nerve that picks up sensations in your face. In response, blood vessels throughout your head quickly contract, then dilate again, and it's thought that this sudden change is what causes the ice cream headache.

Short of giving up frozen treats, what can you do to avoid brain freeze? Next time you're eating something cold, trying keeping it closer to the bottom of your mouth so you don't trigger the temperature-sensitive nerves in the roof of your mouth. And if you do experience a sudden ice-induced pain, placing your tongue against the roof of your mouth to warm it up can help put everything back to normal.

— CHAPTER 1 FAST FACTS —

- DIGESTION BEGINS IN YOUR MOUTH, RIGHT FROM THE MOMENT YOU TAKE THAT FIRST BITE OF FOOD.

- **SALIVA** CONTAINS **ENZYMES** THAT HELP BREAK FOOD DOWN INTO DIGESTIBLE BITS BEFORE IT MOVES FARTHER INTO THE GUT.

- ENZYMES ARE SPECIAL MOLECULES THAT SPEED UP CHEMICAL REACTIONS, AND EACH KIND OF ENZYME PERFORMS ONE SPECIFIC JOB. YOUR MOUTH CONTAINS HELPFUL **BACTERIA** THAT AID DIGESTION.

- THE **SOFT PALATE** AND THE **EPIGLOTTIS** WORK LIKE FLAPS TO KEEP YOUR FOOD MOVING DOWN, NOT INTO YOUR WINDPIPE OR UP AND THROUGH YOUR NOSE!

- YOUR GUT HAS ITS OWN NERVOUS SYSTEM—THE **ENTERIC NERVOUS SYSTEM**—WHICH MEANS YOU CAN EAT AND SWALLOW WITHOUT THINKING ABOUT IT.

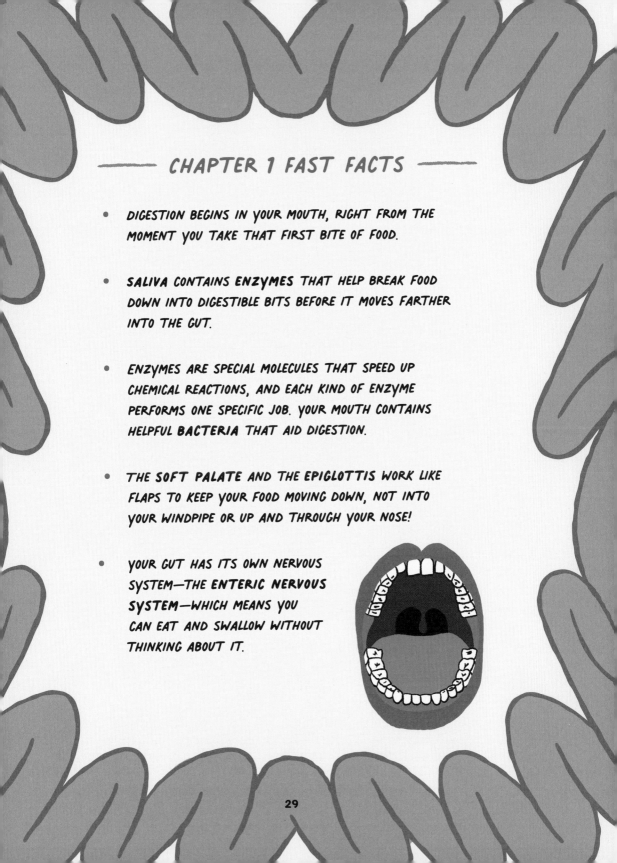

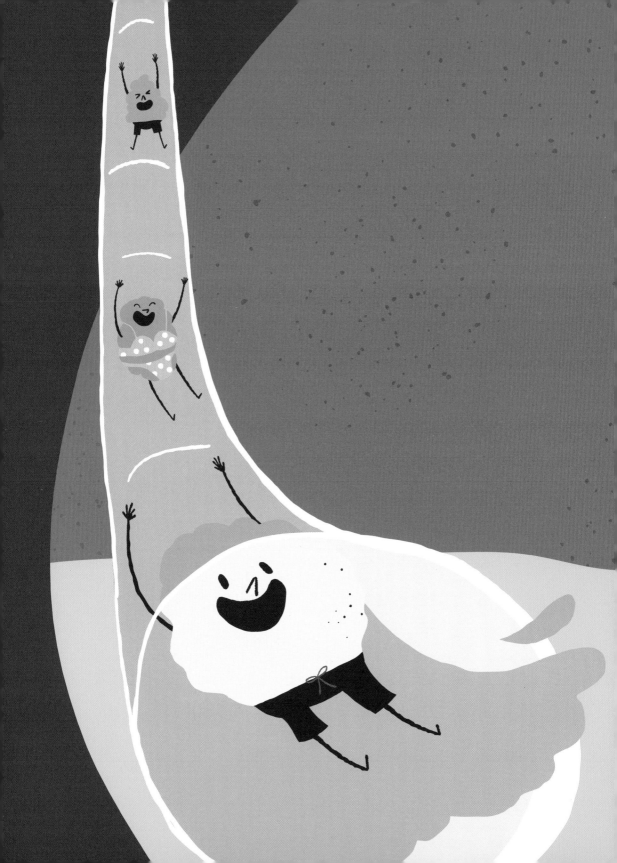

2.

THE
FOOD TUBE

—— YOUR ——
ESOPHAGUS

HOW IS YOUR DIGESTIVE SYSTEM like a worm? No, this isn't a riddle. It turns out that your gut and an earthworm are remarkably similar, and what they have in common is the phenomenon of **peristalsis**. Peristalsis happens when a long, tubular muscle contracts and relaxes bit by bit—it looks a lot like the wave that passes through the crowd at a stadium. Earthworms use this to move along the ground, and your gut uses it to move its contents along.

Peristalsis: "Waving" Goodbye to Your Food

AFTER YOU SWALLOW, the mushy blob of chewed food and saliva makes its way slowly down your esophagus. This tube is roughly 10 inches (25 centimeters) long—about as long as a piece of loose-leaf paper—and the food moves down it slowly but surely, at about 1 to 2 inches (3 to 5 centimeters) per second. It's so slow that you can sometimes feel a bite of food working its way toward your stomach. If your enteric nervous system senses the food has gotten stuck, it'll kick-start a second peristaltic wave in an effort to dislodge the little straggler and keep it going on its merry way.

Peristalsis is a powerful process. Think about it for a moment. If gravity were the only thing forcing food down our gullets, we wouldn't be able to swallow upside down, and astronauts in zero gravity wouldn't be able to eat at all. Gravity helps—it's definitely easier to swallow something when we're right side up—but these magical muscular contractions ensure that we're able to eat, no matter which way we're facing.

That being said, our esophagus isn't a particularly strong muscle. In one of the more unusual experiments done in the name of understanding our guts, scientists tied pieces of food to one end of a string and tied small weights to the other end. Volunteers swallowed the food pieces, leaving the weights dangling outside their mouth to provide resistance. It turns out that it doesn't take very much weight to overcome peristaltic power. Less than half an ounce (as little as 10 grams) of counterweight—about as much as a pencil weighs—was enough to keep the esophagus from being able to swallow the piece of food.

Get Down and Stay Down! The Role of Sphincters

WHILE THE ESOPHAGUS'S MAIN JOB is to move food down to your stomach, it also has another important duty: keeping things from coming back up! The process isn't always perfect—more on that later—but with the help of a special type of muscle, most of what you eat has a one-way ticket through your gut.

A **sphincter** is a ring-shaped muscle that tightens and relaxes, opening and closing whatever tube it surrounds. Along the entire length of your gut, you'll find six sphincters. The one you're probably most grateful for is at the very end of the line—the one that keeps poop in until you've found a toilet—but don't underestimate the other ones!

The first two sphincter muscles in your gut mark the beginning and the end of the esophagus. The upper esophageal sphincter opens and closes when we swallow and is part of the machinery that helps direct food one way and air the other. The lower esophageal sphincter lets food pass into the stomach, but it also keeps the contents of your stomach—including stomach acid—from coming up. Have you ever heard someone say they have heartburn? It has nothing to do with their heart. Instead, it's all in the esophagus. If a little bit of stomach acid escapes through the sphincter, it can cause this uncomfortable burning sensation.

What about the other four sphincters? In order, they're the

- pyloric sphincter, the gateway from the stomach to the **small intestine**;

- sphincter of Oddi, which allows **bile** (see chapter 5) and digestive enzymes into your gut;

- ileocecal sphincter, which opens and closes the passage between the small and **large intestine**; and

- anal sphincter, which is actually two sphincters for the price of one. The inner sphincter holds poop in, while the outer sphincter, which you can relax voluntarily, lets poop out.

THE ODD SPHINCTER

The sphincter of Oddi was named for Ruggero Oddi (1864–1913), an Italian anatomist. He was only 23 and still a student when he became the first to describe how this special muscle worked. He gave his name to a disease too—if this muscle is inflamed, you have "odditis"!

What Can the Circus Teach Us About the Esophagus?

MOST PEOPLE DON'T THINK MUCH about their esophagus—it's just that chute that gets food into our stomachs. But there's one very small group of people—only about 100 of them in the entire world—to whom this simple tube is a matter of life and death... sword-swallowers.

If you've been to a circus, you might have seen the amazing feat that is sword-swallowing. A daredevil leaps onto the stage and in front of a partly terrified, partly disgusted audience, thrusts a long sword down their throat, all the way up to the hilt. It's no trick, either—X-rays have shown that the sword really is inside their throat, with the tip sometimes reaching as far as their stomach! What's their secret? Well, the key to sword-swallowing is... not swallowing.

For over 4,000 years, professional sword-swallowers have been training themselves to completely relax their throat. They wrest control of their sphincter muscles away from their enteric nervous system, and seem to be able to control them at will. By tilting their head back and letting these muscles go slack, they can create an almost perfectly straight tube from their mouth down to the entrance to their stomach, making their esophagus into a sort of sheath for the sword. This takes incredible practice, and most of these daredevils begin by learning to suppress their **gag reflex**.

Our throats are constantly looking out for things that shouldn't be there, and when they detect the presence of something that's not food, they automatically contract to force the object out. This is our gag reflex, and you've probably had it happen to you when someone's put a tongue depressor a little too far back in your mouth. Sword-swallowers (or maybe we should call them throat-relaxers) spend years training themselves to ignore this reflex by swallowing all sorts of objects that do not belong in their mouths, starting with small things and working their way up to larger and larger objects. Do NOT try this at home.

All that practice pays off, both for these daredevils, who now have a pretty cool trick they can take on the road, and for us too—we can thank sword-swallowers for a lot of what we know about the esophagus. These days, it's very easy for a doctor to use a small camera to look inside our guts—a process called **endoscopy**. But in the 19th century, this sort of technology didn't exist. Instead, a German physician named Adolf Kussmaul built a tube—about as long as from your elbow to your farthest fingertip—lined with mirrors and containing a small lamp, designed to provide an inside view of the esophagus. It was far too bulky for any normal person to swallow, but Kussmaul found a sword-swallower willing to help. His experiments provided the first views of the esophagus inside a living person, and ultimately led to the type of specialized cameras doctors use to peer inside of us today.

CHAPTER 2 FAST FACTS

- FOOD MOVES THROUGH THE **ESOPHAGUS** AND INTO THE STOMACH.

- YOUR GUT MUSCLES PERFORM WAVE-LIKE CONTRACTING AND EXPANDING MOTIONS CALLED **PERISTALSIS** TO MOVE FOOD ALONG.

- **SPHINCTERS** ARE RING-SHAPED MUSCLES THAT OPEN AND CLOSE YOUR DIGESTIVE TUBES.

3.

ENZYMES AND ACID AND MUCUS, OH MY!

— INSIDE — THE STOMACH

POINT TO YOUR STOMACH. Now look down and see where your finger is. If you're like most people, you're probably pointing at the middle of your abdomen, maybe a little higher than your belly button. You're a bit off the mark, though—your stomach is actually much higher up and on the left side of your body, under your heart and lungs. When you think you've got tummy trouble, you're usually feeling something amiss farther down the line.

Your chewed food enters the stomach after a rough ride. It spent the last 10 inches (25 centimeters) or so of its journey being slowly squeezed downward through the esophagus—and now it enters a large, comfortable chamber, with room to spare. The stomach isn't just a big hollow sac, though. It's actually shaped a little like a bean, with a short side on top and a longer side on the bottom. This unusual shape helps the stomach organize its workload.

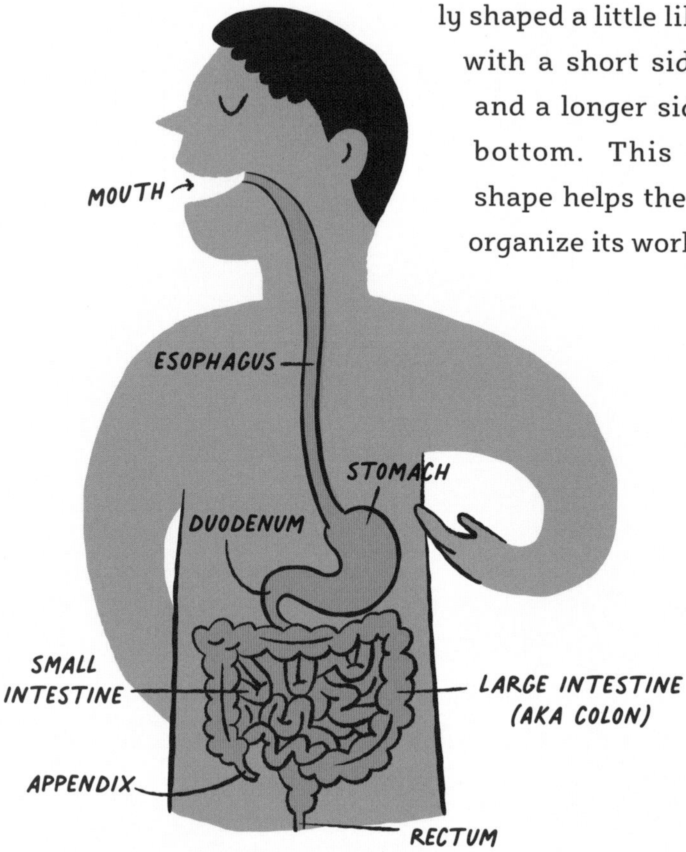

MOUTH →

ESOPHAGUS

STOMACH

DUODENUM

SMALL INTESTINE

LARGE INTESTINE (AKA COLON)

APPENDIX

RECTUM

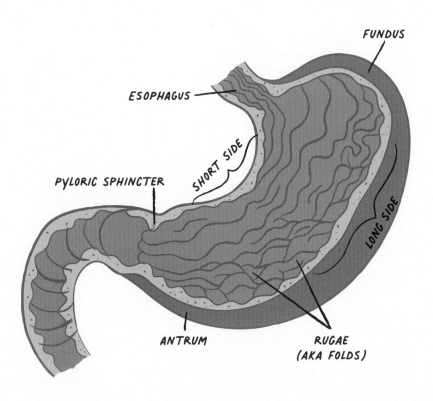

FUNDUS

ESOPHAGUS

SHORT SIDE

PYLORIC SPHINCTER

LONG SIDE

ANTRUM

RUGAE
(AKA FOLDS)

Think about doing your homework. Do you start with an easy assignment, tackling it quickly, so you can spend more time on the harder stuff? That's what your stomach does, thanks to its unique shape. Much of what enters the stomach is liquid, which can be moved directly to the small intestine. Food is a little trickier, though. It needs to stop and stay awhile, so the stomach can break it down into small enough pieces to move down the line. The long side of your stomach-bean contains lots of folds that trap the food, holding it in place until it can be liquefied by stomach acids, while the short side allows liquids to pass through right away.

Filling Up

NOT ONLY DOES THE STOMACH have an unusual shape, it also has remarkable stretching power! When it's empty, your stomach can hold only about 2 or 3 ounces (75 milliliters) of food and liquid—that's about five swallows' worth, less than a big glass of juice. When you eat, though, your stomach can expand to over ten times its original size and hold as much as 4 cups (1 liter) of food and drink! Thanks to the enteric nervous system, your stomach knows when food is headed its way, and that's its cue to relax and get ready to expand. It's also why when you're worried or nervous you tend to eat less—your stomach can't relax to its full capacity.

Have you ever eaten so much that you thought your stomach might burst like a balloon? Don't worry—it can't, for many reasons. First, when your stomach expands to take in a big meal, it's not inflating like a balloon. Instead, those folds that help trap your food and hold it simply stretch out. Second, unlike a balloon, your stomach has an exit—a hatch leading to your small intestine. Things are always moving forward, especially liquids, so not everything you take in is spending a lot of time in your stomach. And finally, thanks again to your enteric nervous system, your stomach can sense when it's getting too full and send a signal to your brain saying "STOP! No more food!"

Usually you get the "I've had enough" message long before your stomach reaches its maximum stretch capacity. But some people are able to override the warning. Think about competitive eaters—people who train for years to be able to eat massive quantities of food in a single sitting. One of the biggest competitive eating events is held in New York City every July 4, with contestants battling to see who can eat the most hot dogs in ten minutes. The most recent champions have all eaten over 70—that's at least seven hot dogs a minute—so their stomachs needed to expand to hold about 2 gallons (over 7 liters) of hastily chewed wiener and bun mush! For them, eating that much food is simply a matter of "mind over meal."

How Does the Stomach Work?

SO, WHEN YOUR CHEWED FOOD drops into the stomach, what does it meet? It's actually a churning, sloshing sea of acid strong enough to burn through wood or metal!

In the 19th century, scientists disagreed about how the stomach worked. Some claimed that the stomach's muscular contractions mechanically ground up food into smaller and smaller pieces until they were tiny enough to pass into the small intestine. Others believed that the process had to be chemical—that churning alone couldn't explain how the food got so small. Some said both—just as a washing machine needs both detergent and tumbling power to clean your clothes, your stomach digests food both mechanically and chemically.

The answer to the question came thanks to an unusual twist of fate.

In 1822, a fur trapper named Alexis St. Martin was shot by a musket, a type of gun that fires a large ball. The ball tore a hole through his abdomen into his stomach. Miraculously, he survived; however, the wound never closed properly. Dr. William Beaumont was treating St. Martin and noticed that whatever food his patient ate would soon appear through the hole that remained in his side. Beaumont recognized an opportunity to observe digestion in action.

Over the next 11 years, Beaumont conducted hundreds of experiments, everything from tying food to a string and leaving it in St. Martin's stomach for varying periods of time, to licking the inside of his patient's stomach to determine when it began to produce digestive juices. (As a scientist who's looked at digestion, I can assure you that we DON'T do stuff like this anymore!) While disgusting, Beaumont's experiments proved that digestion is largely chemical in nature, though the churning of the stomach contents helps speed up the process. And Beaumont was the first to deduce exactly which chemicals make up our digestive juices.

Recipe for Gastric Acid

Your stomach produces many compounds:

- **Mucus** to lubricate the stomach wall and protect it from acid

- Enzymes that continue the digestion process that began in your mouth

- **Hormones**—chemical messengers—that tell your brain when you're full

But perhaps the most important is **hydrochloric acid** (HCl). HCl is used for many things out in the world, from household cleaning to taking the rust off steel, but in your stomach, it has just two jobs: to break down the proteins in the food you've eaten to start the digestive process, and to kill any bacteria that might be hitchhiking on your food to make you sick.

The walls of your stomach secrete other chemicals too, and when these mix with the HCl, we call the whole mixture **gastric acid**—and it sure is acidic! It's similar to lemon juice or vinegar. And your stomach can make about 6 cups (up to 1.5 liters) of gastric acid every day!

If you've ever used vinegar to dissolve the grime from an old coin, you might be wondering why all this gastric acid doesn't eat away at the walls of your stomach. The answer lies in one of the other compounds your stomach produces—**bicarbonate**.

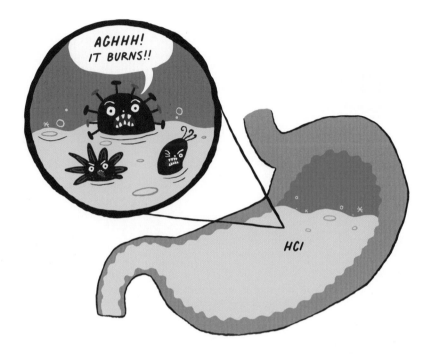

You've probably seen bicarbonate before—if you've used baking soda in the kitchen, you've used bicarbonate. But you might not have known how important a role it plays in your own body. Bicarbonate is a base—the opposite of an acid. And the expression "opposites attract" doesn't really apply to acids and bases. In fact, when an acid encounters a base, a chemical reaction changes both of them into something different. The acid is neutralized, turned into harmless water and salt. Your stomach produces small amounts of bicarbonate to keep the gastric acid at just the right pH balance—acidic enough to help digest food, but not so strong as to irritate your gut.

Hormones:
Your Gut Messengers

Your stomach starts producing gastric acid as soon as you see a tasty meal in front of you, and it's all thanks to your enteric nervous system. Your brain, eagerly anticipating the imminent deliciousness, sends a "Food is coming!" signal along the vagus nerve—the longest nerve in your body, which runs from your brain all the way to your gut. When that signal reaches your stomach, it tells the cells lining your stomach wall to start producing **gastrin**.

Gastrin is a hormone—a chemical compound that acts as a sort of messenger, telling your body to do something. In this case, gastrin tells the cells lining your stomach to start making HCl because food is on its way. It's a bit like a relay—the first message your stomach gets says "Make gastrin," and the gastrin then sends a message saying "Make HCl."

Your stomach produces other hormone messengers too. One of these, **ghrelin**, is known as the "hunger hormone" and it's produced when the stomach is empty. It sends a signal to the brain saying "Feed me!" When you finally eat and your stomach begins to expand to accommodate the food, the stretching motion of your stomach cues your body to stop making ghrelin, and you feel satisfied. All these chemicals and hormones work together in a complex balancing act—"I'm hungry!" "I'm full!" "This is acidic and dangerous!" "Don't worry, we can neutralize this!"—with the end result being that you eat just the right amount, and your stomach is ready to handle it all.

The Beat of Your Gut

Chemicals are clearly important, but you can't overlook the role that your stomach's muscles play in helping to break down your food too. In the same way your heart beats, your stomach beats too, only a lot more slowly—about three times per minute. This helps to create the contractions that churn food about, exposing it to the gastric juices. These contractions are what you're hearing when your tummy rumbles. Although we tend to think of only empty stomachs as being growly, the truth is that they're growling all the time. You just hear them better when your stomach's empty and the growl is amplified.

The Dessert Stomach, Explained

Why is it that even after a huge, filling meal you can still somehow find room for dessert? The answer was discovered only recently, and it came as quite a surprise to many people. It turns out that your stomach can taste!

The same taste receptors that are found in your taste buds can be found in your stomach. Scientists think this is how people develop a preference for energy-rich foods—the stomach recognizes the value of these foods and teaches us to seek them out.

Sweet foods like dessert may not be good for you, but they sure do pack a sugary punch. Our bodies developed at a time in human history when food was often scarce, and sweet foods represented extremely valuable sources of energy. So, when a sweet

treat hits your stomach, it triggers the taste receptors there that produce the hunger hormone ghrelin. Even though you might be full, that first bite of dessert has overridden your brain and is telling you to go ahead and eat more in order to fuel up on energy.

BUTTERFLIES IN YOUR TUMMY

Just what are "butterflies in the tummy," that strange sensation you get in your gut when you're nervous about something?

You've probably heard of the "fight-flight-freeze" response—your body's built-in system to protect you from danger. When you sense a threat, without even thinking about it you stay and fight, run away, or freeze in place.

When you're nervous, this response is triggered. Your body produces a rush of the hormone adrenaline, causing blood to flow away from your gut and toward your limbs in case you have to use them to escape danger. It's this lack of blood flow to your stomach and intestines that gives you that queasy feeling.

Time for Chyme

DEPENDING ON THE TYPE of food you've eaten, it might be tossed and turned in your stomach for hours. Liquids pass through fairly quickly, while **carbohydrates**, like cookies and cake or potatoes and pasta, might spend two hours or more tumbling about. Proteins, like meats, take even longer to break down—around six hours.

Eventually, that blob of chewed food becomes something else—a mushy substance we call **chyme** (pronounced "kime"). At this point, it's no longer recognizable as food. The bits of cake and cookie and steak are tiny now—less than one sixteenth of an inch (2 millimeters)—and they are bound together by water, bits of mucus, and gastric acids, so they look more like sludge than food. And although it might look like it's gone through the digestive blender, chyme is still technically only partially digested food. Most of the real work of digestion will take place in the small intestine, the next stop on our journey through the gut.

CHAPTER 3 FAST FACTS

- YOUR STOMACH PRODUCES LOTS OF **HYDROCHLORIC ACID** TO BREAK DOWN FOODS AND KILL BACTERIA, **BICARBONATE** TO BALANCE OUT ALL THAT ACIDITY, AND **MUCUS** TO PROTECT THE STOMACH LINING.

- THANKS TO THE ENTERIC NERVOUS SYSTEM AND CHEMICAL MESSENGERS CALLED **HORMONES**, YOUR STOMACH KNOWS WHEN TO GET READY TO DIGEST AND WHEN TO STOP EATING.

- YOUR STOMACH TURNS FOOD INTO A MUSHY SUBSTANCE CALLED **CHYME** BEFORE THE MUSH MOVES ON TO THE SMALL INTESTINE.

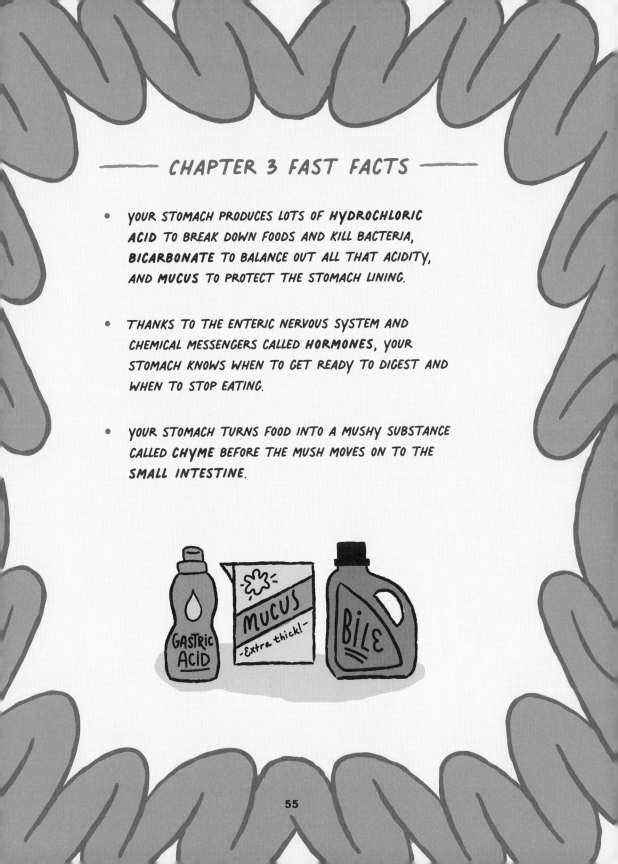

4.

WHEN WHAT SHOULD GO DOWN COMES UP AGAIN

THE SCIENCE OF BARFS AND BURPS

BEFORE WE TRAVEL FARTHER down the digestive tract, let's take a moment to explore the science behind what happens when what went down insists on coming back up. How do we barf and burp?

Barfing

NOBODY LIKES TO BARF, and for good reason—it means something is wrong. Maybe you're sick, maybe you're anxious, maybe a roller coaster put your tummy in a tizzy; something happened, and that something is making your lunch come back up again.

Vomiting is how your body responds to an emergency alert from your gut, and it happens in stages—let's call them BarfCon One, Two, and Three.

BarfCon One is nausea—that vague feeling in your gut that something is wrong. It's caused by tension in your gut muscles, and it doesn't necessarily mean you're going to puke—sometimes it goes away on its own. If it worsens, we move to . . .

BarfCon Two—retching. Your abdominal muscles and the muscles you use to breathe contract rapidly, causing little coughs and spasms. Again, you might stop here, although once you start retching, the odds are pretty good that you're about to spew.

BarfCon Three—vomiting. As gross as it is, barfing is quite an intricate process. It starts with physical cues: sweating, a swiftly beating heart, and a rush of blood to your gut that makes you look pale. You begin to produce lots of saliva—your body knows that you're about to forcibly expel the highly acidic contents of your stomach, and it wants to protect your tooth enamel.

Next, you take a deep breath and close off the entrance to your airway, ensuring that whatever comes up goes straight out and not back down into your lungs.

Beginning in the small intestine, you experience a **retroperistaltic wave** (that's a backward peristalsis, with your gut pushing your food upward instead of downward). Your stomach and esophagus and all their various sphincters relax. And then, with a great push from your diaphragm and abdominal muscles, the contents of your stomach (and even your small intestine, which is why you can puke on an empty stomach) are forcibly ejected at great speed up and out of your body, ideally into some sort of waiting receptacle.

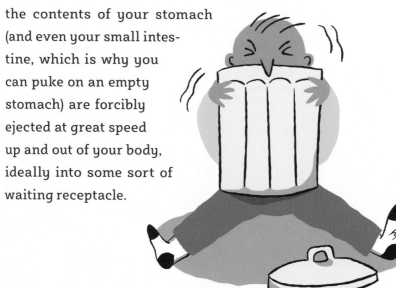

Why Do We Barf?

BLUURCH!

A lot of things can cause us to barf. Germs
are one of the major culprits. A virus, like
norovirus, can bring on vomiting extremely quickly—one minute you might feel
fine, then moments later you're bent over
a toilet bowl, having progressed through
all three BarfCon stages in mere minutes.
Other bad bugs, like the bacteria that cause
food poisoning, tend to cause a slower buildup,
giving you much more time to find the nearest
toilet. Sometimes nervousness causes vomiting. And so
does motion sickness: riding in a car or on a roller coaster
can be a barfy experience for many people.

You might even throw up just because you see someone
else puking! Humans and other primates, like chimps and
gorillas, are the only animals that experience this sort of
chain-reaction barfing. Scientists believe that it's because
we are often eating similar meals, whether it's humans gath-
ered around the family dinner table or primates foraging
in the same part of the jungle. If one member of the group
suddenly takes ill, there's a good chance that everyone else
ate something bad too, so it's best to get it out of the system.

Fortunately, barfing is a relatively rare occurrence—
many people can go years without throwing up. But very
few of us can go more than a few hours without releasing
something else . . . gas.

PUTTING THE BRAKES ON BARF

If you feel like a little retroperistalsis is about to ruin your day, what can you do to stop yourself from barfing? Everyone has their own suggestions, but these are some of the most common ones:

- Take a medicine designed to prevent nausea and vomiting.

- Touch your P6 point. In traditional Chinese medicine, applying firm but gentle pressure to a spot on the inside of your wrist, about three fingers' width below the wrist joint, is a remedy for nausea. You can even buy a little wristband with a button on it that will keep pressing on this special spot.

IN CASE OF NAUSEA, PRESS HERE!

- Chew on a piece of ginger or suck on a ginger candy.

- Keep your eyes locked on the horizon. If you're feeling motion sick thanks to a wild roller-coaster ride, a car ride, or a rocking boat, looking straight forward can make things better.

BUUUURP!

*...MY COMPLIMENTS
TO THE CHEF!*

Burping

BURPING, OR BELCHING, is what happens when your stomach releases gas. Unlike a fart, which is stinky gas produced by the bacteria in your intestines (see chapter 7), a burp is usually odorless and is simply made of gas that you've swallowed. It might be air you gulped while you were eating, in which case the burp is made up of nitrogen and oxygen, or it could be carbon dioxide from a fizzy drink.

A burp begins when an air bubble forms in your stomach and pushes upward, triggering the sphincter that separates the stomach from the esophagus and telling it to open. The air bubble rockets upward, moving quickly through the pharynx and past the vocal cords (that's what causes the burp sound), and then out it comes, likely followed by an "Excuse me!" Burping isn't considered bad manners everywhere, though—in certain parts of the world, burping after a meal is how you express your appreciation to the chef! And some people really know how to express their appreciation. The loudest burp on record was nearly 110 decibels, about as loud as a jackhammer hammering away right next to you!

SPACE BURPS

Next time you burp, take a moment to think about the astronauts orbiting the earth aboard the International Space Station. A lot of things are tricky to do in space—move around, sleep comfortably, go to the bathroom—but did you know that burping is also a challenge? On Earth, the gas in our guts floats, hovering over the mush in our stomach. But in zero gravity, that gas is mixed in with a lot of damp food sludge, so when a burp is expelled, it brings a little of that grossness along with it. Astronauts even have a special word for this half-burp/half-barf: *bomit*. Bet they don't teach you about that in astronaut school.

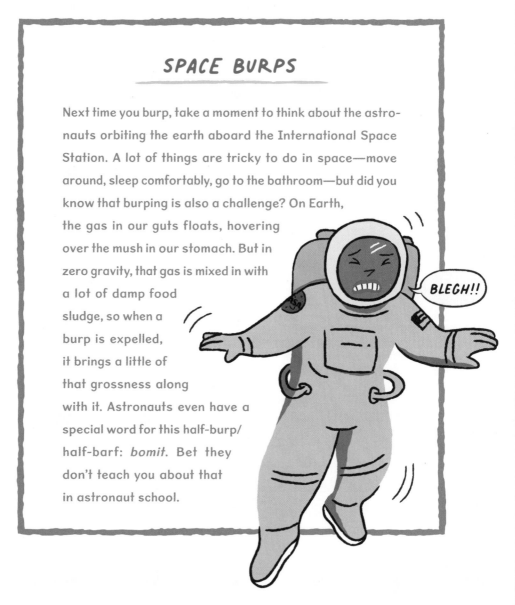

BLEGH!!

Hiccups

HIC! HIC! HIC! They may be annoying (especially for one poor fellow who lived with a case of the hiccups for 68 years!), but to many scientists, hiccups provide a fascinating insight into human history.

A hiccup is an involuntary contraction of the muscles that help you breathe, especially the diaphragm. This spasm triggers your vocal cords to snap shut, resulting in that characteristic *hic!* sound. Hiccups often happen when you've eaten too much or too quickly, had a fizzy drink, or swallowed some air, which can happen when you gasp with excitement. They tend to go away on their own in a few minutes, though everyone seems to have a favorite trick for curing them quickly, from having someone scare you to drinking water upside down.

We start hiccupping in the womb, as early as eight weeks after conception. And it's not just humans who hiccup—all mammals do it. Scientists interested in human evolution have spent a lot of time thinking about why we hiccup. One group of researchers thinks that hiccups are a leftover from breathing the way certain amphibians do, using both lungs and gills. Others think that hiccupping developed so that the first mammals could burp out the air they swallowed while drinking their mother's milk. Still others think hiccups evolved to help us clear food stuck in our esophagus.

CHAPTER 4 FAST FACTS

- MANY THINGS CAN MAKE YOU VOMIT, FROM BACTERIA AND VIRUSES TO NERVOUSNESS TO MOTION SICKNESS.

- VOMITING HAPPENS WHEN THE BODY INITIATES A **RETROPERISTALTIC WAVE**, AND EVERYTHING THAT GOT PUSHED DOWN GETS PUSHED BACK UP AGAIN.

- A BURP IS A BUBBLE OF AIR FROM THE STOMACH THAT ROCKETS UP THROUGH THE **PHARYNX** AND PAST THE VOCAL CORDS, MAKING A TELLTALE SOUND!

- A HICCUP HAPPENS WHEN THE MUSCLES THAT HELP YOU BREATHE QUICKLY CONTRACT, USUALLY AFTER YOU'VE SWALLOWED A LOT OF AIR.

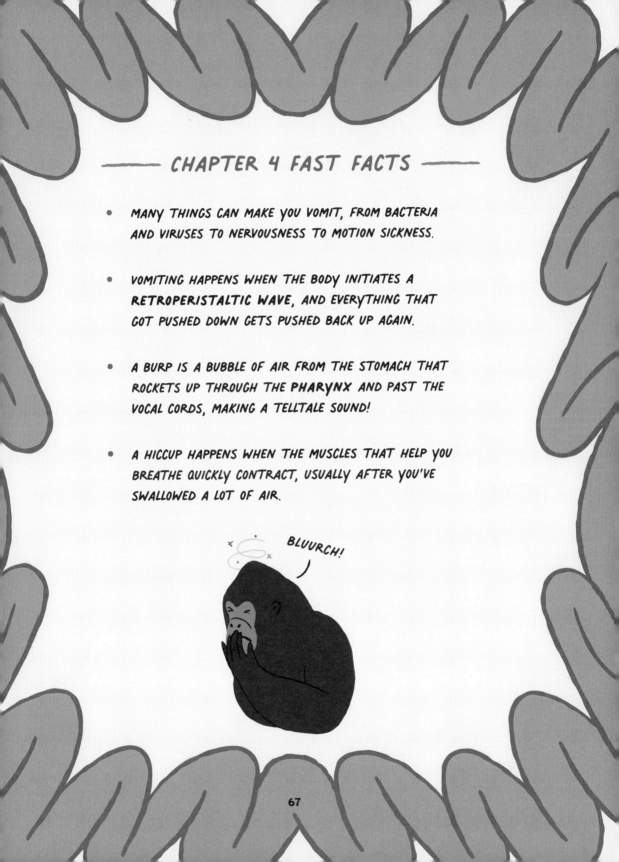

BLUURCH!

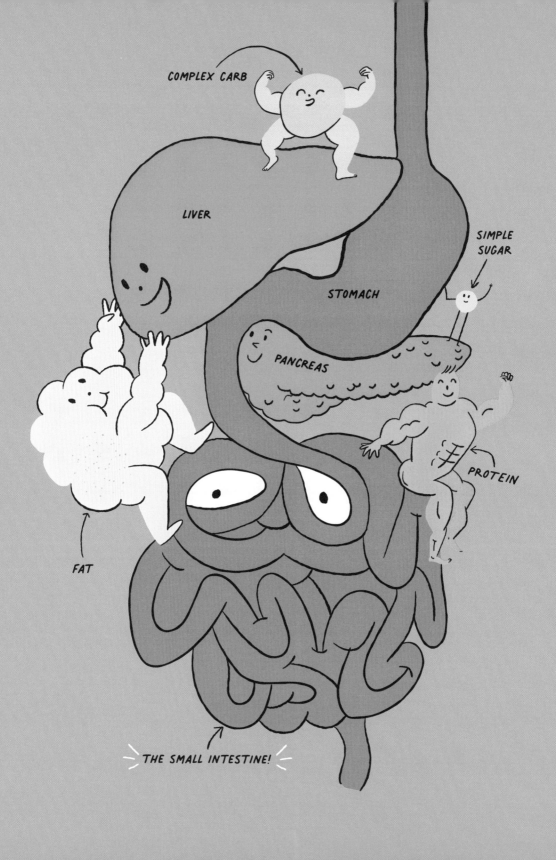

5.

DESTINATION DIGESTION

THE NOT-SO-SMALL INTESTINE (AND FRIENDS)

THE SMALL INTESTINE IS anything but small. While it may have a narrow diameter, about as big around as an adult's finger, if you uncoiled this snake-like mass of guts, you'd find it stretches anywhere from 10 to 16 feet (3 to 5 meters) long—the taller the person, the longer the small intestine. In fact, across the animal kingdom, most animals have a small intestine that's about three and a half times their body length. That means a blue whale's can be 500 feet (150 meters) long!

Lovely
Lengthy Loops

THERE'S A LOT HAPPENING in all that length of intestine.

1. The first foot (30 centimeters) or so is called the **duodenum**, and this section has two very important jobs. First, it acts as a gatekeeper—it sends a hormonal signal to the stomach saying "The small intestine is ready! Send in the chyme!" This signal opens up the pyloric sphincter, and in comes the chyme. Its second and perhaps most important job is to gather the many enzymes needed for digestion and get to work breaking down your food.

2. The next part of the small intestine is the **jejunum**, which does most of the work of absorbing nutrients from the digested food.

3. The last part is the **ileum**, which plays an important role in your immune system.

How do all those guts fit inside of us? While we're in the womb, they don't! For a brief period during our embryonic development, our small intestine grows so quickly that it pokes out of the body and into the umbilical cord. It tucks itself back in place only once the embryo's abdomen has grown large enough for it. Eventually, we develop a sort of web-like structure made of tissue and blood vessels that tightly packs all that tubing into one compact spot, a bit like a net holding a bunch of helium balloons in place.

The inside of the small intestine might appear smooth to the naked eye (I've seen mine with a camera and it sure looked pink and shiny). But if you zoomed in to take a closer look, you'd find that it's actually covered with millions and millions of tiny, finger-like projections called **villi**, each a tiny fraction of an inch (about 1 millimeter) in length. These villi dramatically increase the surface area of your small intestine. In fact, if you were to stretch every single little villus out and lay it flat, you could cover an entire tennis court!

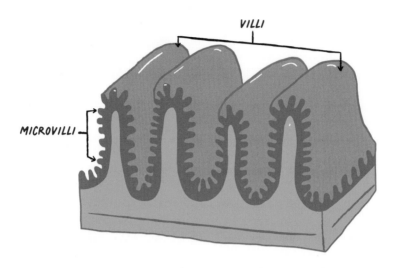

VILLI

MICROVILLI

The reason for this is simple. The point of digestion is to get nutrients out of the food you eat, and the small intestine is where almost all of that takes place, so the more surface area your gut has, the more nutrients you can extract from your food. That chyme that just left your stomach? By the time it's traveled through the small intestine, 95 percent of it will have been broken down further and absorbed into your body, providing the nutrients and energy we need to survive.

The small intestine also absorbs water—a LOT of water. Every day, we drink about 4 to 8 cups (1 to 2 liters) of liquid. But our digestive system produces even more than that—about 1.5 to 2 gallons (6 to 7 liters) of secretions like saliva and gastric acid. All this water has to go somewhere, and much of it—about 80 percent—is reabsorbed by the small intestine, passing through the cells of the villi and directly into the bloodstream.

The -Ums

THE WORD *DUODENUM* COMES from a Latin phrase meaning "12 fingers' width" because it's about... 12 finger-widths long! But a lot of important work happens in that small space. The duodenum controls the pace of digestion. It opens and closes to let the contents of your stomach carry on their journey through your gut. Over the course of an hour, peristalsis helps move chyme from one part of the small intestine to the next. At the same time, it acts like a sort of mixing bowl by collecting juices secreted by other organs, like the liver and the pancreas, that will help break down the chyme even further. It also adds bicarbonate to help neutralize any stomach acid that might have snuck in.

The jejunum is where your body extracts most of the nutrients it gets from food. In fact, by the time chyme has traveled the 6 feet (2 meters) of this tube, your body has absorbed 90 percent of the nutrients in your food! Millions of cells lining the folds of your jejunum act like sponges, soaking up the tiny molecules released as you digest your food and turn proteins, fats, and sugars into the nutrients and energy your body needs. If you look at these cells under a microscope, they look as if they have hair! It's not actually hair, though—instead, it's those little projections, or villi, that give the cells more surface area for absorbing.

The cells of the ileum, the last 6 to 13 feet (2 to 4 meters) of the small intestine, look hairy too. This is where any last

THE -UMS

DUODENUM

JEJUNUM

PEYER'S PATCH ON THE JOB

ILEUM

nutrients that weren't absorbed earlier make their way into your body. But the ileum has another important job besides absorption. Your gut is essentially one long tube, from your mouth to your butt, and it's open at both ends. Because that leaves it exposed to the outside world, it's going to encounter germs. The bacteria-fighting compounds and acids in your mouth and stomach take care of most of these, but the occasional bad bug can slip through. Your ileum is covered in special patches of cells, called **Peyer's patches**, where immune cells are standing on guard, looking for invaders and ordering your body to destroy them.

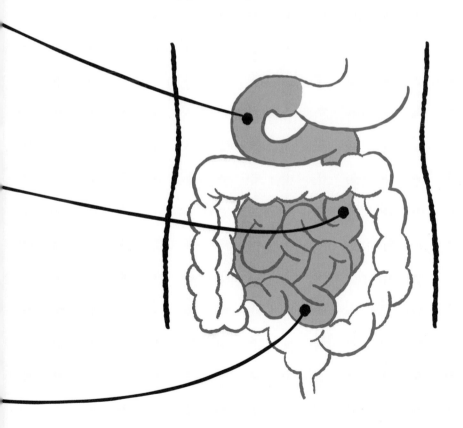

From Food to Fuel

SO NOW WE KNOW what happens to our food as it passes through the small intestine, but how it's digested is slightly more complicated. Just as all humans look very different from each other but are built from the same basic building blocks, so too is all the food we eat assembled from a common set of molecules. Whether it's a cookie, an egg, a turkey dinner, or a grilled cheese sandwich, all of our food is made up of sugars, protein, fat, or some combination of those three. And each of these is absorbed by the body in a slightly different way.

Sugars

Sugars are found everywhere in our diet. Sugar isn't just the sweet stuff we eat in candy form. A more complex carbohydrate, like a whole wheat pasta noodle, is broken down to the same thing, sugar. The only difference is in how long it takes—pure sugar is absorbed fairly quickly, while more complex carbohydrates have to be broken down into smaller and smaller molecules by many different enzymes. There are a few sugar compounds that humans can't digest, though. Ever seen a corn kernel in your poop? The outside of the kernel is made of cellulose, which is a type of sugar that our bodies can't break down. We can get at some of the material inside the corn kernel, but the outer skin passes through our systems unscathed.

The sugars that we can absorb, like glucose and fructose, enter the hairy cells in the small intestine through special transporter proteins, little gates in the walls of the cells that recognize one very specific molecule and grant it passage. The sugar molecule drifts through the cell, and when it reaches the other side it passes right into the bloodstream.

A SUGAR BY
ANY OTHER NAME

What's the difference between sugar and a carbohydrate? When it comes to visiting the grocery store, the answer seems obvious. Sugar is, well... sugar. It's white and granular, or sometimes powdery, and it comes in a bag or a box, and eating a bunch of it can make us act a bit wacky. Carbohydrates—or carbs, for short—are in foods like bread or pasta. The science of sugars and carbs is a little more confusing, though. Let's break it down.

All sugars are carbohydrates (molecules made of carbon, hydrogen, and oxygen), but not every carbohydrate is a sugar. The sugar we're used to using in baking or in the sugar bowl is called **sucrose**. Like some of the other sugars you may have heard of (glucose, fructose), sucrose is a sweet-tasting molecule that can dissolve in water. This family of molecules is sometimes called simple sugars, or simple carbohydrates, and while they give us energy, that's about it—they don't give us any other nutrition. It's a good idea to minimize the

sugar in our diet by taking it easy on things like candy and soda. That doesn't mean we have to eliminate carbohydrates, though.

Complex carbohydrates are an important part of our diet. These molecules—which include the starch we get from foods like potatoes and the fiber we get from many plant foods—provide both energy and nutrients. Because these molecules are much bigger than simple sugars, they take longer to digest and help our body maintain an even level of energy, rather than the sugar high we might get from choosing a sweet treat over whole-grain bread.

MILK MUTANTS

Baby mammals, whether human or animal, get their nutrition from one food source—milk. Milk is rich in the sugar lactose, but in order to provide energy for our growing bodies, it has to be broken down by an enzyme called **lactase**.

As babies, we all produce lots of lactase. However, as we grow older, we make less and less of it, and by the time we're five to ten years old, we hardly make any of it at all. The same thing happens in baby animals—it's nature's way of telling us it's time to be weaned off our mother's milk.

Without lactase, lactose passes to the large intestine, where bacteria break it down and produce gas. This causes the symptoms that we describe as "lactose intolerance"—gas, bloating, and pain.

Not everyone is lactose intolerant, though. Many people actually produce lactase throughout their life and can digest milk and cheese with no problem. We can thank a marvelous mutation for this.

Long ago in human history, around the time that humans started to raise cattle, someone, somewhere had a mutation in their genetic code that meant they never turned off their lactase factory. This gave them the ability to drink milk from their cows, which in turn gave them energy, more energy than their neighbors who didn't have this special mutation.

When a trait gives one member of a population some sort of advantage like this, evolution ensures that the trait spreads to other people in the population. So, over many, many generations, more and more humans were born with this mutation. Today, most people with European ancestry keep making lactase for their entire life, allowing them to enjoy dairy products without fear of digestive distress.

Proteins

The hairy cells lining your intestine also absorb the molecules you get from the protein you eat. While the initial work of protein digestion begins in the stomach, the fragments of protein found in chyme are broken down even further in the small intestine. First, they're broken into small fragments called *peptides*, and then they are broken down again into molecules called **amino acids**.

Amino acids are like the building blocks of life. Think about a set of toy building bricks—there are many different sizes and shapes of bricks, and when you put them together, you can build anything you put your imagination to. Similarly, there are many different types of amino acids— we humans use 21 of them—and they can be arranged in many ways to build all sorts of proteins to give our bodies structure, from the collagen in our skin and bones to the myosin that helps our muscles flex.

Fats

Fats, once they've been broken down by fat-eating enzymes, take a slightly different route into your body. They don't travel through a transporter into a cell and out the other side into a blood vessel. Instead, the tiny molecules you get from digesting oils and fats enter a different type of vessel, called a *lymphatic vessel*.

Your body's **lymphatic system** is a lot like its circulatory system—lymphatic vessels run throughout your body carrying a very important fluid. It's not blood, though—it's lymph, a clear fluid that acts sort of like a subway system for various molecules. Sometimes, lymph carries invading bacteria that your immune system's cells have trapped; other times, it carries away the garbage your cells and tissues make. During digestion, it carries fat away from the small intestine. The fat molecules eventually enter your bloodstream once they hit the end of lymph subway line, and it's a good thing they do—gram for gram, fat gives your cells over twice as much energy as sugars or proteins do.

Where do all the digestive enzymes that turn your food into fuel come from? Although they're not technically part of your digestive tract, there are two organs without which digestion would be impossible—the lovely liver and the practical pancreas.

How Is Your Liver a Lot Like Soap?

YOUR LIVER IS AN incredible organ that performs hundreds of different functions, from making red blood cells to storing vitamins to producing hormones. One of its most important jobs, though, is making bile.

Bile might sound vile, but it's an incredibly useful liquid. Every day you make over 2 cups (half a liter) of this greenish-brown fluid, which is immediately shipped off to another helpful organ—the gallbladder—for storage. Bile is mostly water—about 97 percent—but that other 3 percent contains some useful stuff, like bile acids.

BILE!

Bile acids behave like the molecules that make up something you see every day: soap. Soap works by trapping dirt inside tiny bubbles—not the ones you see when you lather up your hands, but smaller bubbles, invisible to the naked eye. Bile acids form these same sorts of tiny bubbles, called *micelles*, and as it turns out, this is a very useful property when it comes to digesting fat.

You've almost certainly heard the phrase "oil and water don't mix," and it's true—just try adding oil to water and see what happens. Given that your digestive tract is full of water, it makes sense that the oils and fats you eat won't easily dissolve. You have to get at them some other way, and that way is through bile acids.

FAT

BILE ACID

The bile acids mix with the oils and fats you're digesting in a process called **emulsification**. They grab little bits of the fat blob and trap them inside micelles. This makes the fat molecules more accessible to the enzymes that break down fats into smaller and smaller compounds until they can be absorbed by your small intestine.

The
Pancreas

THE PANCREAS IS A small, pear-shaped organ that hides behind the stomach. Its job is to behave like a factory. Your pancreas produces a whole bunch of different enzymes that are able to break down starches, proteins, and the fats that the bile acids have so thoughtfully emulsified. It's these enzymes that are the true workhorses of the digestive system. They break down chyme into progressively smaller and smaller molecules, until your food has become nothing more than a bunch of different chemical compounds, each small enough to be absorbed into your body. The pancreas produces up to 6 pints (3 liters) of digestive fluid, rich in these enzymes, every day, and they empty into your small intestine through the sphincter of Oddi.

Your pancreas also produces two hormones that help to control your body's blood sugar—**insulin** and **glucagon**. Remember how the carbohydrates you eat get turned into sugars like glucose and absorbed into your bloodstream? That's how your body gets energy. But too much or too little glucose can be dangerous. Insulin and glucagon work together to ensure you have just the right amount of sugar in your blood. The pancreas makes glucagon when it senses your blood sugar levels are too low—the glucagon sends a message to your liver to turn stored sugar into glucose. When glucose levels start to increase, your pancreas stops making glucagon and instead produces insulin. This hormone sends the opposite message to your liver—it says, "Take some of this glucose and store it away for the future."

WOULD YOU LIKE A NAP WITH THAT?

Have you ever eaten such a big meal that instead of dessert all you wanted was a nap? Almost everyone has experienced the "food coma" phenomenon, but scientists still can't agree on what exactly causes it. Here are some of their ideas:

- After eating, blood rushes to our digestive system to help us process our meal. This decreases blood flow to the brain, and we get tired as a result.

- Like animals, when we're hungry, we're awake and alert, ready to look for food—a leftover from our hunting and gathering days. Once we've eaten, we can rest and digest.

- Meals rich in protein contain the amino acid tryptophan, which makes us sleepy.

- Other researchers think that the reason we get sleepy after lunch, in particular, has nothing to do with digestion. Instead, it's our body hitting one of its natural energy lows, one that tends to happen around 2 p.m. for most people.

The Origins of Allergies

SNIFFLING, SNEEZING, ITCHINESS—IT MIGHT seem as if allergies come from our noses! Surprisingly, though, their origin often lies somewhere else... our small intestine.

When we're young, our immune system learns to recognize our food as something it will see often, and not an enemy invader that it must defend against. Immune systems are complicated, though, and if something goes wrong during this learning phase, we might end up mistaking a harmless food ingredient for something more dangerous. The next time we see that food, and every time after that, our immune system mounts an attack, and that attack is what we call an allergic reaction.

Scientists think that sometimes, early in life, a bit of undigested food somehow sneaks out of our small intestine into our blood or lymph. It eventually reaches our immune system, where this misinterpretation can happen. Some of the biggest culprits? Milk, eggs, peanuts, tree nuts, seafood, shellfish, soy, and wheat.

What might seem like an allergy, though, is sometimes actually an intolerance to a particular food. Or it can be another disease altogether. Take gluten, for example. Gluten is an umbrella term describing many proteins found in grains like wheat and oats. These proteins give dough its stretch, but they can also trigger unpleasant reactions in some people. In some cases, this might be an actual allergic reaction to one of the proteins. Other people have gluten sensitivity—they find that when they eat gluten, they might get bloated, pass a lot of gas, have aches and pains, and otherwise feel unwell. But the consequences are much more serious for people with celiac disease—after eating gluten, their immune system begins to attack their own bodies, especially the lining of the intestine.

Cleaning Up

BY THE TIME CHYME has reached the end of the small intestine line, there's not much of it left. In fact, the small intestine is pretty clean! I've been lucky enough to get to swallow a tiny camera and see what my gut looks like inside, and I can tell you that, apart from a few floating strings of mucus here and there, it actually looks fairly empty. That's because your small intestine cleans up after itself!

Once peristalsis has finished and the chyme has been mostly digested, the small intestine kicks off a series of powerful muscular contractions—a sort of super-peristalsis—that sends a big cleaning wave down its entire length. This wave pushes any last stragglers or undigested food bits toward the large intestine—the last stop on the journey of digestion.

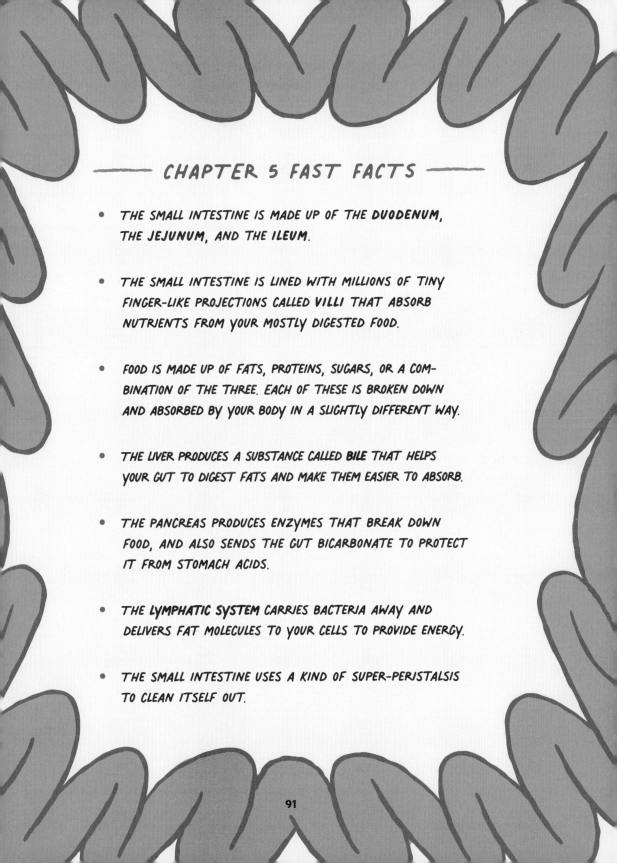

CHAPTER 5 FAST FACTS

- THE SMALL INTESTINE IS MADE UP OF THE DUODENUM, THE JEJUNUM, AND THE ILEUM.

- THE SMALL INTESTINE IS LINED WITH MILLIONS OF TINY FINGER-LIKE PROJECTIONS CALLED VILLI THAT ABSORB NUTRIENTS FROM YOUR MOSTLY DIGESTED FOOD.

- FOOD IS MADE UP OF FATS, PROTEINS, SUGARS, OR A COMBINATION OF THE THREE. EACH OF THESE IS BROKEN DOWN AND ABSORBED BY YOUR BODY IN A SLIGHTLY DIFFERENT WAY.

- THE LIVER PRODUCES A SUBSTANCE CALLED BILE THAT HELPS YOUR GUT TO DIGEST FATS AND MAKE THEM EASIER TO ABSORB.

- THE PANCREAS PRODUCES ENZYMES THAT BREAK DOWN FOOD, AND ALSO SENDS THE GUT BICARBONATE TO PROTECT IT FROM STOMACH ACIDS.

- THE LYMPHATIC SYSTEM CARRIES BACTERIA AWAY AND DELIVERS FAT MOLECULES TO YOUR CELLS TO PROVIDE ENERGY.

- THE SMALL INTESTINE USES A KIND OF SUPER-PERISTALSIS TO CLEAN ITSELF OUT.

6.

MEET YOUR MICROBIOME

THE TRILLIONS OF
— TINY TENANTS —
HELPING YOU POOP

EVEN WHEN YOU'RE ALL BY YOURSELF, with no one else around... guess what? You're never really alone when you have bacteria to keep you company! Every moment of every day, there are billions of bacteria in you, on you, and around you. These bacteria are part of your **microbiome**—the many microscopic organisms, or microbes, living in and on you. Thousands of different species of helpful bacteria can be found all over the human body, and together they're so important to your health and well-being that some people say your microbiome is really an organ, just like your brain, lungs, and heart.

The Gut Microbiome

BACTERIA CAN DIGEST CERTAIN MOLECULES you can't, so when those bacteria are hanging out in your gut, it's a win-win situation—they get a cozy home and delicious food, and you get the nutrients and energy they produce. In fact, about 10 percent of all your nourishment comes from the work of your tiny tenants. Your trusty sidekicks do three important things for digestion:

- They break down carbohydrates you can't digest on your own so that you can use them for energy.

- They produce vitamins that you need.

- They help you to absorb minerals like calcium and iron.

Your *bowel*—that's the term we use to describe the whole intestine, or sometimes just the large intestine—is home to 99 percent of your body's bacteria. That's over 100 trillion cells, representing hundreds of different species. Every time you poop, you lose a few billion of your best friends. The average poop contains hundreds of times more bacterial cells than there are people on Earth! Over the years, thousands of these microbially rich poops have been analyzed in the name of science, and what we've learned is incredible.

Scientists wanted to find out more about all the jobs our microbes really do, and so they designed an experiment. They raised mice under special laboratory conditions, ensuring that they never acquired any microbial companions. Without gut bacteria to help them digest their food, the microbe-free mice were super-skinny, and they had to take in much more food than a typical mouse to maintain their body weight. They also needed a special diet supplemented with the vitamins that gut bacteria normally produce.

The mice raised without microbes had fewer villi in the lining of their intestines. But that's not all. Their immune systems were weaker. And there were differences in their behavior as well: they reacted to stress and anxiety

EXHIBIT A
MICROBE-FREE

very differently from normal mice; they seemed less interested in social situations and making mouse friends; and they groomed themselves repeatedly, like a sort of nervous tic. But here's the thing. All of those effects were reversed... by giving the mice back the microbes they lacked.

Roll Call

IN THE LAST FEW YEARS, scientists have developed new tools to take a microbial head count and see just what types of bacteria live in the various parts of our bodies. Previously, microbiologists could identify only the bacteria that they could grow in their laboratories. Imagine trying to grow all the bacteria from a poop sample. Because a petri dish in a lab is a long way off from a nice, warm, cozy bit of intestine, only a few bowel bugs would ever grow on the dish, and none of the other species could be identified. But now, some very cool lab techniques tell us almost instantly which bacterial species are present in a particular part of the body, even if we can't raise them on a petri dish.

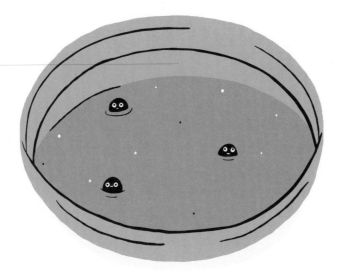

This ability to study the previously hidden microbial world led to a huge study, starting in 2007, called the Human Microbiome Project. Over 200 people volunteered thousands of samples—swabs from their mouths, noses, skin, and other sites, along with plenty of poop samples to get at the gut microbiome. The scientists who studied them found a remarkably rich ecosystem.

Scientists learned that each body site has its own characteristic population of microbes. And we're all quite different from each other—we share only about a third of our bacterial best friends with other people. In fact, our microbiomes are almost as unique as our fingerprints! And while the specific bacteria in your body might be very different from the bacteria in mine, the jobs those bacteria do are remarkably similar, like digesting food and protecting us from harmful germs.

Making Bacterial Friends

YOUR MANY MICROBES ARE your oldest friends. The moment you're born, you pick up a collection of bacterial companions. Exactly which ones move in depend on what route you took out of your mom—passing through the birth canal gives you a healthy dose of *Lactobacillus* and *Prevotella* species, while a surgical C-section exit through the abdomen means you pick up some of the bacteria commonly found on skin, like *Staphylococcus* and *Propionibacterium*. Very quickly, more friends join the party, from the environment, from the many people cuddling adorable newborn you, and from the milk or the formula that you drink.

Many of your first gut microbes are there to help you make the most of the milk you drink. As you grow older and begin to eat solid foods, you have to add more microbial helpers capable of digesting things like fruit and vegetable fiber and the meat proteins you're now munching on. By the time you're about three years old, your gut microbiome has reached its own version of adulthood—it's matured enough to be able to handle almost anything that comes its way. There's a downside to sorting all this out so early, though—if you don't grow a good gut microbiome in your first few years, you might feel the long-term health consequences for the rest of your life.

Sometimes, the problem is that we don't get enough microbial diversity early on. There is such a thing as being too clean, believe it or not. Eating a bit of dirt, getting licked all over by the household doggy, growing up with lots of outdoor play—all of these things put us into contact with helpful microbes that can become part of our own microbial ecosystem. They also help our immune system learn the difference between friendly microbes and harmful ones. When we're too clean, not only are we missing out on microbial diversity, but we also run the risk of having an immune system that doesn't quite work right. A lack of microbial diversity early in life—even as early as a few days after birth—might eventually lead to an autoimmune disease. Instead of fighting germs, the body thinks its own cells are invaders that it must fight off, causing issues like allergies and asthma.

Other times, our microbiome starts off in good shape, but then something goes wrong. Our gut bacteria are generally pretty hardy. Spicy food? No problem. Bout of diarrhea? No big deal. A week spent eating nothing but hot dogs? Got it under control. Our microbial world generally returns to normal pretty quickly. However, if something *really* big comes along and throws the system off balance—like taking **antibiotics** that wipe out lots of our friendly gut bugs—we might lose a lot of our microbial diversity and never recover it.

Not Just Nourishment

AS WE GROW INTO healthy adults, the surface area of our intestine grows too, giving us more room for marvelous microbes. Their duty goes far beyond simple digestion, though—our microbiome is an important part of our immune system.

Plenty of bad bugs can find their way to your gut, but one of the ways your microbial friends keep you safe is by forming a protective coating. The good bacteria that help you digest your food work their way into the mucus that lines your gut to create a protective barrier, physically preventing any bad bugs that might survive their trip through the stomach from finding a way into your body. They also stimulate the production of molecules that your immune system uses to fight off invaders that do get through, lending a helping hand when you have an infection.

BAD BUGS

Our food and water are generally very safe. However, the occasional bad bug can get into our system through the things we eat and drink. If that germ makes it past our many defenses, we might find ourselves experiencing some not-so-pleasant symptoms, like vomiting and diarrhea. Here are a few of the rude dudes in foods that we might encounter:

- **Salmonella:** This bacterium often hangs out in raw eggs or chicken; 12 to 72 hours after eating it, you'll know.

- **Campylobacter:** Found anywhere from chicken to milk to mud puddles, this bacterium can make you sick with cramps and diarrhea for several days.

- **Giardia:** This waterborne parasite causes a disease nicknamed "beaver fever," but there's hardly anything feverish about it—expect two to six weeks of farting and diarrhea.

- **Norovirus:** When people say "stomach flu," they mean noro. This virus spreads like wildfire and comes on quickly. Fortunately, it passes quickly too, but for a few hours to a couple of days, it's best not to stray too far from the bathroom.

ZEN MICROBE

OOOOOHHHMMM...

Microbes can even influence our mood! We've already seen how our gut talks to our brain through nerves and hormones, and it turns out that these conversations can be influenced by our resident microbes. In one study, researchers gave one group of healthy volunteers milk or yogurt enriched with friendly *Bifidobacterium* and *Lactobacillus* bacteria every day for 30 days. The other group was given a placebo—a pill that did nothing. At the end of the month, the group that took the bacterial pill reported fewer bad moods and stressful moments, and they were even producing less cortisol—a hormone produced when you're under stress—than they were at the start of the experiment.

Another experiment looked at students who were about to take a stressful exam. Those who took *Lactobacillus* every day for the two months leading up to the exam had much lower cortisol levels the day before the exam than the placebo group. (No word on whether they scored better on the test, though!)

Poop Transplants

THE HUMAN SUBJECTS WHO ate yogurt were *far* luckier than some of the mice involved in microbiome experiments. The mice had to swallow a mouthful of poop so scientists could see if it would change their microbiome! As gross as that sounds, these studies revealed that by transferring some of our microbiome to another individual, we can make *their* gut start acting like *our* gut!

In 2013, researchers conducted an experiment on human twins. One twin was extremely lean and the other was quite obese. They collected poop from both twins and transferred it into two sets of germ-free mice. All the mice ate exactly the same diet, but weeks later, the mice who had received the lean twin's poop sample weighed less and had less fatty tissue than the mice whose poop came from the obese twin! This got researchers thinking that maybe we could treat certain medical conditions with microbiome therapy, and thus was born the idea of the poop transplant. This isn't a new idea, though. History shows us that many different cultures used poop—human, and even camel—to treat diarrheal diseases.

Diarrhea usually passes quickly, both out of your butt and out of your system, but in some people, it never stops. Multiple medical conditions can cause permanently problematic poops, as can an out-of-balance microbiome. One of the toughest types of diarrhea to treat is caused by this sort of imbalance. Most of our guts have a little colony of a bacterium called *Clostridium difficile*, or *C. diff* for short, which just sort of hangs out—our gut microbiome keeps it from growing out of control. If we disrupt our microbiome, though, often through a course of antibiotics, sometimes that *C. diff* will seize its chance to spread and quickly take over. This sort of infection can be dangerous, even fatal, and it can also be hard to treat with traditional medicines. So, what's a doc to do? A poop transplant.

Known as **fecal microbiome transplants**, or FMTs, this process involves taking feces (poop) from a healthy donor and transplanting it into someone with bad bowels. This can be done via a freeze-dried poop pill that the patient swallows, a poop smoothie that we send into the patient's gut via a tube, or even a synthetic poop substitute, filled with good microbes, that the patient swallows. FMTs are proving so popular, there's now a stool bank! Just like a blood bank, which stores blood from healthy donors, a stool bank stores fecal samples from folks with healthy guts. One of the biggest stool banks contains samples from tens of thousands of donors. And there's even an animal equivalent, storing perfect poops from pets!

Fecal transplants have been remarkably successful in curing persistent poop problems. In some trials, FMTs cured over 90 percent of *C. diff* infections. And so some desperate people have even tried doing their own FMTs at home. This is a terrible idea, though. Poop transplants performed by doctors, using stool banks, are done very carefully, as they don't want any germs transferred from donor to recipient.

Doctors are also not sure about the long-term safety of the transplants. Some unusual side effects have been observed. Like the study with the mice, there have been reports of FMT recipients gaining weight if their feces came from an overweight donor, and some recipients have said that, after their transplant, their taste in food changed. This is surprising, but it hints at the possibility that poop transplants might be useful for more than just difficult diarrhea. One day, they might be used to treat anything from obesity to stress!

Feeding and Caring for Your Microbiome

SO, HOW CAN YOU feed and care for your very important microbiome, helping it to be the best companion it can be?

- Eat many different types of foods to cultivate microbial diversity in your gut, especially plant foods. Fruits and

DELICIOUS YOGURT!

vegetables that are high in fiber, or whole grains, are some of your gut bacteria's favorite things to digest. They also love molecules called *polyphenols*, which you can find in extra-virgin olive oil, dark chocolate, blueberries, and many other foods. Fermented foods are also a great choice—things like yogurt, kimchi, and sauerkraut all contains lots of helpful *Lactobacillus*.

• Avoid heavily processed foods—the kind where you don't recognize most of the words on the ingredient list.

Probiotics, Prebiotics, Antibiotics ... What's With All the Biotics?

PROBIOTICS ARE LIVE BACTERIA that are thought to be good for your health. They come in many forms, but usually they are sold as foods—like yogurt laden with *Lactobacillus*—or as capsules filled with friendly *Bifidobacterium*. By giving yourself an extra helping of helpful bacteria, the thinking is that you'll get more of the benefits good gut bacteria have

ANTIBIOTIC RESISTANCE

Germs are very clever and are able to fight back against antibiotics. Of the billions of bacteria in your body, if just one is somehow able to resist the antibiotic treatment, it'll be the only one to survive and pass its resistance on to the next generation. Very quickly, what was a simple infection becomes untreatable. The problem of antibiotic resistance is one of the most serious threats facing doctors today, and scientists are racing against the clock to discover new antibiotics before time runs out on the ones we have now. This is why it's so important not to take antibiotics unless we really need them.

to offer, like helping to digest your food, keeping your gut safe from other germs, and even preventing diarrhea.

There's a lot of uncertainty around **probiotics**, though. Scientists are still trying to figure out exactly how they work and which bacteria are best for particular jobs, and the medical industry is still studying how safe they are. That being said, humans have been taking probiotics via food for thousands of years. Fermented foods, like yogurt, kimchi, and some soy sauces, have been filling our guts with beneficial bacteria for a very long time.

Unlike probiotics, **prebiotics** aren't actually bacteria; instead, they're foods that are thought to help probiotic bacteria to grow. Think of prebiotics as a meal for your gut microbiome. By giving the beneficial bacteria in your bowels their favorite treats, you're helping them to multiply and thrive. They love fiber, so lots of veggies is the way to go if you want to help your probiotic bacteria grow.

Antibiotics are very different—these are medicines that kill bacteria. Sometimes that's a good thing. Since they were first used almost 80 years ago, antibiotics have saved millions of lives by curing dangerous infections. But antibiotics can also do more harm than good in some cases. They often kill the good bacteria in your gut along with the bad bacteria they're supposed to be attacking, and this can cause temporary diarrhea. If your bowel bacteria don't bounce back, you might be at risk for a more serious illness, like *C. diff.*

CHAPTER 6 FAST FACTS

- YOUR GUT IS HOME TO HUNDREDS OF DIFFERENT SPECIES OF BACTERIA THAT HELP YOU DIGEST YOUR FOOD AND ALSO SUPPORT YOUR **IMMUNE SYSTEM**.

- YOU START PICKING UP GUT BACTERIA AS SOON AS YOU'RE BORN, AND THE MORE DIVERSE YOUR GUT BACTERIA ARE, THE BETTER!

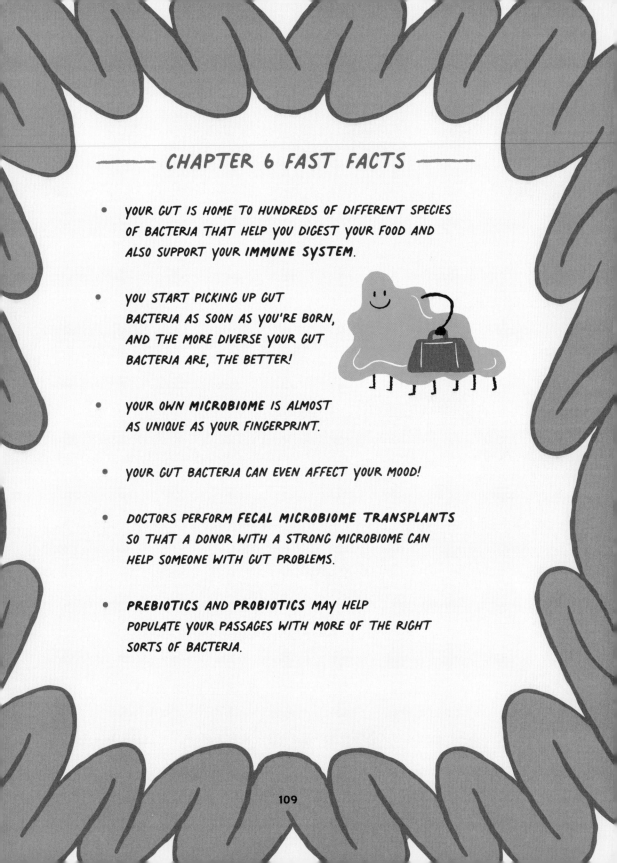

- YOUR OWN **MICROBIOME** IS ALMOST AS UNIQUE AS YOUR FINGERPRINT.

- YOUR GUT BACTERIA CAN EVEN AFFECT YOUR MOOD!

- DOCTORS PERFORM **FECAL MICROBIOME TRANSPLANTS** SO THAT A DONOR WITH A STRONG MICROBIOME CAN HELP SOMEONE WITH GUT PROBLEMS.

- **PREBIOTICS AND PROBIOTICS** MAY HELP POPULATE YOUR PASSAGES WITH MORE OF THE RIGHT SORTS OF BACTERIA.

7.

PERISTALSIS AND POOP

THE LARGE INTESTINE

THE LARGE INTESTINE IS the fecal factory, the place where poop is produced—as much as a pound (half a kilogram) of it every day. Stool, waste, feces, number two, doo-doo—whatever you want to call it, this is where it comes from. But before what's left of our food assumes its final form, the large intestine has to take care of a bit of, er, business.

The Many Jobs of the Large Intestine

THE LARGE INTESTINE IS actually shorter than the small intestine—the word "large" refers to this tube's diameter, not its length, which is just 5 feet (1.5 meters). By the time what's left of the chyme has reached this last stop on its journey, most of the nutrients and around 90 percent of the water from your food and drink have already been absorbed into your body. So, what's left for this little stretch of gut to do?

First, your large intestine needs to deal with any undigested food that somehow made it out of the small intestine, like some of the carbohydrates that the enzymes in your digestive juices can't handle. The large intestine doesn't produce any of its own digestive juices. Instead, it gets at these additional nutrients with the help of your gut microbiome. These beneficial bacteria help you make the most of your meal by doing a bit of the digestion work for you. Nutrients and vitamins released by your faithful microbial companions can be absorbed by the cells lining the large intestine.

Just as large is the opposite of small, the lining of the large intestine is completely opposite to the lining of your small intestine. There, we saw millions of little outward projections called villi; here, there are millions of little indentations, called **crypts**. A tiny area of your large intestine—around the size of one of the periods on this page—contains about 100 crypts, and when you add them all up, you're looking at around 10 million tiny dents in total. The cells in the crypts help your colon with its other jobs—moving things along, and drying things out.

THE USELESS APPENDIX?

The dictionary defines an appendix as "supplementary material at the end of a piece of writing." It's like extra information that the reader can choose to read or not (and by the way, this book doesn't have one!).

Your digestive tract has an appendix too—a tiny tube about 4 inches (10 centimeters) long located at the start of the large intestine. This appendix got its name because scientists couldn't figure out what it did. It seemed like an extra organ that people didn't really need and only noticed if it became inflamed and had to be removed.

But it turns out the appendix may be pretty useful after all. Scientists think that the appendix may be a small storage chamber housing beneficial bacteria. If your gut microbiome is somehow disrupted, your appendix can reseed it with these friendly microbes.

Around twice a day, your large intestine makes a big peristaltic push, shoving the now unrecognizable remnants of your meal ever closer to the exit. It's slow but steady progress—it might take anywhere from 12 hours to several days for a poop to form and work its way out. And it takes a few turns too. The tube that is your large intestine first goes up, then it goes over, and then down, so that powerful push helps your proto-poop to take those corners. Mucus, produced by the cells in your millions of crypts, greases up the tubes to help out, and the mucus itself ends up as part of the poop.

Ever wonder why you sometimes have to poop not long after you've eaten? It's because of that peristaltic push. The act of eating a meal, especially a large one or one that's rich in fatty foods, triggers your large intestine to start pushing. The large intestine can also send poop back up the line by pushing in reverse, which is helpful when you just can't get to a toilet.

The large intestine also acts as a dryer, with the cells in each crypt absorbing almost all of the remaining water from the chyme. This is the magical moment when chyme becomes poop. When it starts moving through the large intestine, you wouldn't recognize poop as poop—it's more of a clear liquid with bits of undigested food, like fruit and vegetable fiber, floating around. As more and more water is removed, this proto-poop begins to firm up. As it passes along the length of your bowel, it picks up stuff along the way, including mucus and dead bacteria, and by the time it reaches the end of the line, it looks pretty firm and pretty familiar. Sometimes this drying-out doesn't go as planned, though, and the result? The dreaded diarrhea.

Why Is Poop Brown (and Stinky)?

AS YOUR POOP BEGINS to pull together, its brown color becomes more obvious. That lovely shade comes from a yellowish substance made in your liver called **bilirubin**. This is the stuff that gives bruises that ugly yellow color. Bilirubin finds its way into bile, which you'll remember from our journey through the small intestine (chapter 5). In the large intestine, bacteria break the bilirubin down, turning it from a yellowish color to something more brown.

While stool is usually brown, we can poop almost the entire rainbow. Many brightly colored foods, like red beets or blue fizzy drinks, can change the color of our feces, and a common over-the-counter pink medicine for tummy trouble actually has the unusual side effect of turning our poop black!

When we're babies, our very first poop is almost always dark green or black, and it's so special it gets its own name, **meconium**. This poop contains everything we have ingested in the womb: mucus, the fluid that surrounds a developing fetus, even hair—the soft, downy fluff that covers developing babies makes it into their guts! This first poop has an unusual sticky texture, a bit like tar, and unlike the rest of the poops we'll make during our lifetime, it has no odor.

As soon as our guts become home to the bacteria that help us digest our food, just hours after we're born, our poops start to stink. As they break down the chyme in our large intestine, these microbes produce stink molecules. Weirdly, in small amounts these compounds actually smell nice—they're even used in perfumes!—but in large enough quantities, they have a very distinct poop odor. Many other molecules contribute to the stench too, and scientists can actually identify these in the lab. By mixing pure liquid versions of those chemicals together, they can make what is most certainly the worst perfume in the world—synthetic poop stink. Why would anyone make such a thing? As it turns out, fake poop smell is extremely useful when companies are trying to test new sanitation systems or products designed to mask poop smells. Rather than using real poop, they simply mix up a batch of synthetic stink to use in their experiments. Using different combinations of chemicals, scientists have even determined that although what we eat can slightly change the smell of our poop, there's no way to make it smell good.

The Back Door

ONCE YOUR STINKY POOP package is ready for delivery, it heads for the end of the large intestine. Known as the **rectum**, this chamber is a sort of waiting room for poop and farts. A few times each day, your colon pushes its contents into the rectum. Solids, liquids, and gas—it all enters this special place.

FART FACTS

Believe it or not, there's an entire field of study devoted to farts—**flatology**, or the study of flatulence. Some very brave scientists have conducted all sorts of strange experiments in the name of fart science, and they have discovered some fascinating, foul-smelling facts over the years.

Did you know that the average human farts 10 to 20 times every day? Most of that gas is made by the bacteria living in your bowel, although whatever air you swallowed that didn't escape in burp form can become a fart too.

Most of the gases that make up a fart are odorless—things like hydrogen and methane (both of which are highly flammable) and carbon dioxide. Only around 1 percent of a fart is made up of stink molecules, which are usually sulfur compounds produced by the bowel bacteria. Each person's bacterial community is a little different, and the gases it produces depend on our diets, which is why everyone's farts smell a little different, and their smell can change when we eat different foods (beans, brussels sprouts, onions, and dairy are some of the best fart-producing foods). We also quickly get used to the smell of our own farts, which is why you don't gross yourself out every time you toot.

From the silent-but-deadly to the ripper, there's a whole symphony of fart sounds. The volume and tone depend on a lot of things, like how tight your anal sphincter muscle is and how fast and powerfully the fart is moving. Size matters too, and the first fart of the day is usually the biggest, releasing all the intestinal gas that accumulated while you slept.

In the rectum, two very important muscles work together to ensure your poop stays inside until you're ready to go. The internal anal sphincter muscle senses whether your rectum is full or not. When your waiting room is full, this circular muscle relaxes and tells your brain, "It's time. We have to poop." Your external sphincter is the muscle you can thank for being able to hold that poop in until you can reach a bathroom. Unlike the internal sphincter, this gate is under voluntary control. You can hold it closed until you're on the toilet.

That level of coordination is pretty impressive, but what's even cooler is how your body can sense the difference between a poop and a fart. When your guts are rumbling, you intuitively know whether what's brewing is a gas or a solid and whether it's safe to let out a little toot or whether you should seek out a toilet. But how? Your rectum is lined with special sensory cells that can detect what's in the

waiting room. The cells transmit this information to your brain, which is how you sense what's going on down below.

Not only does your brain help with pooping, but so do your lungs! Think about one of the first things you do when you're about to go—you close your airway and breathe out. That straining motion causes your diaphragm to press down on your digestive tract, helping push things along. And push things along it does—poop shoots out of the body at a speed of about an inch (2 centimeters) per second. Remarkably, humans and other mammals all take about 12 seconds to poop, no matter how long our bowels are. An elephant's guts are ten times as long as a cat's, but Jumbo and Fluffy both do their business in the same amount of time.

The shape of your poop depends on how much time it spends in your colon, and scientists have devised a numbering

TYPE 1
SMALL, HARD LUMPS
(LIKE MARBLES)—
HARD TO PASS

TYPE 2
SIZE IS NORMAL,
BUT BUMPY ALL OVER

TYPE 3
MOSTLY SMOOTH,
BUT WITH CRACKS
AND CREVICES

TYPE 4
SOFT AND SMOOTH,
LIKE A FAT SLUG

TYPE 5
SMALL, FLUFFY
DOLLOPS

TYPE 6
GOOPY MUSH, LIKE WET
MASHED POTATOES

TYPE 7
ALL LIQUID—
NO SOLID POOP
TO BE FOUND!

WOMBAT POOP!

system to classify the different shapes. The Bristol stool chart is a scale from 1 to 7, where a 1 indicates poops that are small and hard, like little pebbles, and a 7 is basically water—diarrhea to the extreme. Most people poop out number twos that are 3s and 4s: smooth and shaped a lot like a sausage. Wombats, on the other hand, poop out something that's definitely not on the chart—little poop cubes! These adorable animals—the only ones in the world to poop perfect squares—have an unusual large intestine. It contains two long grooves, and scientists think it's something in the way these grooves stretch when a poop is passing through that lends wombat waste its unusual shape.

While we're on the subject of animal poop (which has many names, from scat to dung to guano, even frass and spraint!), let's all take a moment to be thankful that we're not sloths. Just like the animal itself, sloth digestion is *slooooooow*. It can take up to a month for these tree-dwelling mammals to fully digest a meal. They poop only once each week, but when they do, they make it count. They can poop out as much as one-third of their body weight at a time, and people who have watched sloths poop say you can even see their abdomens shrinking as they do their business. Thankfully, sloths don't poop in their trees, so people trekking through the tropical rain forest don't have to worry about all that sloth poop falling on their head. Instead, sloths climb—slowly—down their tree and do a "poop dance" to dig a little hole, where they very thoughtfully bury their leavings.

THE POWER OF POOP

After the poop you produce has landed in the toilet with a triumphant splash (ideally sinking quickly out of sight—a floating poop can be a sign of too much gas or an overly fatty diet), you might think the story's over. After a few days in your system, whatever you ate has been chewed, swallowed, churned, digested, and pushed out the back door. But scientists are finding all sorts of uses for poop!

Since prehistoric times, people have been burning dried poop—both human and animal—to use for heat and fuel, but this process creates a lot of pollution. Now scientists have figured out how to turn poop into a much cleaner source of power—something called biogas. And it's all thanks to bacteria.

To make biogas, poop is dumped into a big tank containing many different bacteria that turn poop into methane and carbon dioxide gases. These can be used right away as fuel, or they can be transformed into other types of energy. The gas can be compressed into fuel that can power a car, or it can be converted into electricity and used to power a house or a farm, or the electricity can be sent back to the electrical grid to be shared with other people.

NASA is even looking at using poop as rocket fuel. Currently, the space station and the space shuttles store poop temporarily; then, when the bin is full, they eject the poop into space—imagine aliens running into that as their first contact with humans!

Using the same sort of process used to make biogas here on Earth, future astronauts might generate enough methane to power a return trip home—nearly 80 gallons (300 liters) of rocket fuel per crew member per week!

We can even turn poop into clean drinking water. That's the idea behind the Omni Processor, an incredible machine that not only turns waste into water, but also uses energy from the poop to power itself. Fresh poop enters the machine, where its first stop is a dryer. The steam evaporating off the drying poop is collected, and when that water vapor runs through a condenser and filter, it turns into clean, drinkable water. Meanwhile, the dried solid waste can be burned, with the resulting energy used to power the entire machine.

Poops in Space

Pooping can be quite a challenge for humans too, when we find ourselves in unusual situations. Take pooping in space, for example. The first space flights were short, just a few minutes, so NASA engineers didn't give much thought to how to deal with human waste (an oversight that became uncomfortably obvious to one early astronaut, who peed in his space suit). When it came time for longer flights, NASA's solution was essentially just a bag that astronauts would poop into. Despite a sticky adhesive end meant to keep the bag attached to an astronaut's butt, accidents did happen. During Apollo 10's return from the moon, a loose poop escaped and floated around the spaceship, while the three astronauts joked, "Don't look at me—it's not one of mine!"

Eventually, NASA's engineers developed a toilet that made pooping on the space shuttle or the International Space Station much easier. Astronauts preparing for a space mission even spend time "potty training," learning to use these special toilets. But what about during a long space walk? How do you poop inside your space suit? Currently, astronauts wear a very fancy diaper, but NASA recently held a contest—the Space Poop Challenge—to find a better idea. Over 5,000 ideas were submitted by people around the world, and the winning design was a sort of hatch in the crotch of the suit to which various hoses and collectors could be attached.

A Brief History of the Toilet

ALTHOUGH PEOPLE LOVE TO claim that Sir Thomas Crapper invented the toilet, the truth is that humans have been using some sort of system to trap their waste for around 5,000 years. The earliest toilets were simple seats positioned over a chute that would carry waste into a sewer or pit, sometimes with the help of flowing water. This design thrived for thousands of years, and it's still possible to find old castles with this sort of system. It was also common to simply poop in a pot, emptying it every now and then into a sewer or onto fields to be used as fertilizer.

The earliest report of a flush toilet resembling what we use today dates all the way back to 1596. However, it would be another three centuries before flush toilets were produced on a large enough scale to see them used regularly in homes. This is where the perfectly named Sir Thomas Crapper comes in. Although he did not invent the flush toilet, he did design several of the plumbing elements we'd recognize in the toilets of today.

November 19 marks World Toilet Day. Although it might sound like a strange excuse for a celebration, this annual observation is actually meant to draw attention to the fact that over half the world's population doesn't have access to quality sanitation.

The Perfect Pooping Position

Sitting on a toilet to poop is a very strange thing to do. Let me explain. For almost as long as people have roamed the earth, we haven't had toilets to sit on. And even today, any tenacious traveler can tell you that there are a lot of different toilet styles in the world, from the throne-like ceramic seats you might be used to, to tub-like ones you have to squat over. In fact, for almost all of human history, we've been squatting—not sitting—to poop.

Nobody will disagree with the fact that toilets have been a tremendous invention, helping people everywhere poop safely and cleanly, and ensuring that all our waste can be whisked away, keeping our homes and neighborhoods clean.

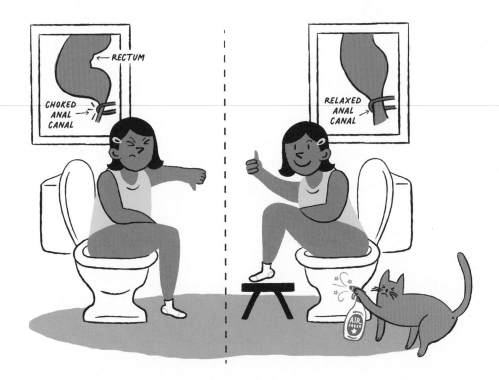

But there is some debate around the best position to poop in, and how toilets can be better designed to help our feces flow.

It turns out that when you're seated, you introduce a bit of a bend into your piping. However, when you squat to poop, lowering your butt below the level of your hips, that last bit of tubing straightens out, providing a much easier exit for your poop. This means that the squat toilets used in many parts of the world are actually a better design than the ones you might be used to. But that doesn't mean you need to rip out your toilet and replace it with a hole in the floor. A small stool or anything else that can raise your knees up while you're seated can help you assume that perfect pooping position.

THE SMART TOILET

Our pee and poo both contain lots of signals that can tell doctors when something is wrong. This is why you may have had to pee into a cup or collect a stool sample at some point when you were feeling poorly. What if we could skip the tricky collection step, save ourselves a visit to the doctor's office, and instead have our toilets diagnose what ails us? This is the idea behind smart toilets.

Although they might look like a regular toilet from the outside, inside they're equipped with all sorts of sensors to detect any unusual signs of distress. Artificial intelligence can then go to work on the data, determining the best course of action: Does your toilet send you to the doctor? The emergency room? Or maybe the local grocery store to pick up a probiotic? In the future, your daily defecation might replace your semiannual checkup.

We can even use poop to fight disease on a bigger scale. By using the same types of sensors in a smart toilet in the sewage system that serves an entire neighborhood, doctors and disease detectives could scan all the waste that a community produces, keeping an eye out for the presence of any dangerous pathogens or anything else that shouldn't be in our sewers. One day, this might help us to identify a disease outbreak more quickly and stop it before it can spread too far, or detect the presence of dangerous drugs or chemicals in our community.

CHAPTER 7 FAST FACTS

- THE **LARGE INTESTINE** PASSES YOUR CHYME ALONG USING PERISTALTIC CONTRACTIONS, AND IT ABSORBS WATER, TURNING THE CHYME INTO POOP.

- IN THE **RECTUM**, THE POOP WAITS UNTIL YOU'RE READY TO GO AND TWO MUSCLES—AN INTERNAL AND EXTERNAL ANAL SPHINCTER—GIVE IT THE ALL-CLEAR TO COME OUT.

- THAT'S NOT THE END OF THE STORY, THOUGH—POOP CAN BE USED FOR FUEL AND EVEN DRINKING WATER!

8.

THE END.

— REALLY. —

YOUR GUT IS SO much more than just a tube. It's a magnificent assembly of muscles, nerves, and microbes that even has a mind of its own. Like a magician, it transforms ordinary objects—cookies, cake, hot dogs—into the extraordinary: energy to power cells, proteins to build a strong body, chemicals that influence behavior. Without your gut, you couldn't survive.

Scientists are only beginning to unlock the secrets of this special system, and many years from now, I'm sure I'll have to write an even bigger book with the latest inside scoop on our insides. But for now, I hope you've enjoyed your journey through your guts and learned to appreciate them—I sure have. Next time your tummy rumbles or a fart slips out, you'll know why it did, and instead of trying to cover it up, be proud—that's your body's coolest organ in action.

Glossary

amino acids: chemical compounds that are the building blocks of proteins

antibiotics: medicines that treat bacterial infections

bacteria: small, single-celled organisms

bicarbonate: a chemical compound that neutralizes acid

bile: a greenish-brown fluid made by the liver that helps digest fats

bilirubin: the compound in bile that gives it its color

carbohydrates: compounds, like sugars, made of carbon, hydrogen, and oxygen atoms

chyme: the mixture of partially digested food and stomach juices that exits from the stomach

crypts: small indentations in the lining of the large intestine

duodenum: the first part of the small intestine

emulsification: the process through which large globs of fat are broken down into smaller ones

endoscopy: a medical procedure that uses a camera to look inside the gut

enteric nervous system: the part of the nervous system that controls the organs and muscles of the gut

enzymes: special proteins that convert one chemical into another

epiglottis: a flap at the base of the tongue that closes to prevent food from entering the trachea

esophagus: the muscular tube connecting the throat to the stomach

fecal microbiome transplant: the transfer of poop from a healthy donor to a person with an intestinal disease

flatology: the nickname for the study of flatulence (farts)

gag reflex: the contracting of throat muscles in response to something touching the roof of the mouth

gastric acid: a mixture of chemicals, including hydrochloric acid, secreted by your stomach

gastrin: a hormone that triggers the release of gastric acid in response to the presence of food

ghrelin: a hormone that causes feelings of hunger

glucagon: a hormone that helps regulate blood sugar levels by triggering the liver to turn stored sugar into glucose

halitosis: the scientific term for bad breath

hormone: a chemical messenger produced in one part of the body that signals another part of the body to take a particular action

hydrochloric acid: a strong acid that is produced in the stomach to assist digestion

ileum: the last part of the small intestine

immune system: the body's defense system against infectious diseases and other threats

insulin: a hormone that helps regulate blood sugar levels by telling the liver to store excess glucose

jejunum: the middle part of the small intestine

lactase: an enzyme that breaks down the sugar lactose

large intestine: the final stretch of the gut, where poop is formed

lymphatic system: the body's system for removing toxins and waste, and for transporting fats away from the small intestine

masseter: a powerful muscle that closes the jaw during chewing

meconium: a baby's first poop

microbiome: the population of bacteria and other microorganisms living in a particular environment, like the gut

mucus: a slimy substance the body produces for both lubrication and protection

peristalsis: the process by which food or chyme is moved along the gut through a series of muscle contractions and relaxations

Peyer's patches: patches of the small intestine lining that are part of the immune system

pharynx: the chamber that connects the mouth to the esophagus, often called the throat

prebiotic: foods that promote the growth of helpful gut bacteria

probiotic: a food or pill containing live helpful gut bacteria

rectum: the end of the large intestine

retroperistaltic wave: peristalsis in reverse, which pushes the contents of the gut upward instead of downward

saliva: the watery liquid produced in the mouth that helps lubricate during chewing and begins the process of digestion

small intestine: the part of the gut after the stomach, where most of the nutrients from food are absorbed into the body

soft palate: the soft tissue at the back of the roof of the mouth

sphincter: a ring of muscle that opens and closes a tube like the esophagus or intestine

sucrose: the sugar commonly used in cooking or in the sugar bowl

supertaster: a person who experiences tastes more intensely than others

taste buds: small patches of tongue cells that are involved in tasting

trachea: the breathing tube that connects the mouth and throat to the lungs

villi: finger-like projections that increase the surface area of the small intestine to aid in digestion

Index

THIS BOOK OFFERS A LOT of information about your gut, and about how your body breaks down and digests everything you eat and drink. But it includes a lot of other really fascinating facts and topics along the way! This index will help you to quickly find the information you are most interested in by showing you what pages to look for it on.

To use the index, look for a key word, like "stomach" or "poop." The key words appear in alphabetical order. The numbers after each key word are the page numbers that you can use to find the information. Page numbers in a range (for example, 6–7) mean that information is found on pages 6 and 7. Page numbers in italics point you toward a picture on the page.

Sometimes you might think of one key word but the information is under a different word, so the index will suggest *See* (for example: barfing. *See* vomiting). Or maybe there's more information listed under a different key word, so the index will suggest *See also* (for example: stomach. *See also* gastric acid). Sometimes it's fun just to take a quick look at the index, because you might find something surprising...like "sword-swallowing"?